WORLD OF YOUTUBE

You did it. You actually bought a one-way ticket and are headed for the World Of YouTube. We hope you're ready cause let us tell you; it's nothing like planet Earth.

wetheunicorns.com's World Of YouTube is the ULTIMATE destination for YouTuber fans. We live to bring you inside access on all of your favourite creators, both big and small. From news to interviews, quizzes to in depth commentary – we've got your back.

So sit back, strap in and take a deep breath – it's gonna be one hell of a ride.

CONTENTS

QUIZ: SHOULD YOU START A YOUTUBE CHANNEL?

You've been thinking about it for a while now, so to help you we've created this handy flowchart that will tell you precisely whether or not you should start your very own YouTube channel – try it out!

ARE YOU ALIVE?

NO

YES

ARE YOU A GHOST?

YES, YES I AM

DO YOU LIKE YOUTUBE?

NO

NO, JUST REAL DEAD

YES

DON'T LIE TO US

HAVE YOU CONSIDERED MAKING A CHANNEL BEFORE?

YES

ARE YOU SHY?

YES

NO

RIP

YES

NO

RIP BRO

HAVE YOU CONSIDERED THAT YOU ARE AWESOME AND UNIQUE AND CAN DO ANYTHING YOU SET YOUR MIND TO?

YES

NOT EVEN A LITTLE?

NOPE

GOOD POINT

LOVE THAT CONFIDENCE

I ALREADY HAVE A CHANNEL

SO, WHAT'S STOPPING YOU?

DON'T MAKE A CHANNEL

MAKE A CHANNEL!

THEN MAKE SOME VIDEOS, DINGUS!

THE TEN COMMANDMENTS (OF YOUTUBE)

YouTube truly is a bountiful gift given to us by the Internet Angels. HOWEVER, that does not mean that we can just do whatever we want on YouTube – there be'eth rules, my friend. The most important of these rules are the mighty Ten Commandments of YouTube, which you should all learn by heart.

YouTube Commandment I
Thou shalt not comment 'First', even if thou art really, really sure thou art first.
Don't be'eth that guy.

FIRST!

YouTube Commandment V
Thou shalt not comment questions about the video before thou hath finished the video.
It's in the video, fool.

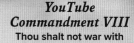

YouTube Commandment VIII
Thou shalt not war with other fandoms.
There be'eth room for all.

YouTube Commandment II
If there is a new video from thine online bae, thou shalt like it before even watching it.

YouTube Commandment VI
Thou shalt not finish a video without asking people to rate'th, comment'eth and subscribe'th.

YouTube Commandment IX
Thou shalt not use suggestive video thumbnails to try and get more views.

YouTube Commandment III
If thou do not like the video, do not watch the video.
Nobody is making thou watch it.

YouTube Commandment VII
If thou like it: click thumbs up. If thou do not like it: do not click thumbs up. If thou hate it. Click thumbs down.
This is important.

YouTube Commandment X
Thou shalt not plaster thy videos in annotations.
People should be able to click to pause.

YouTube Commandment IV
Prejudice and negativity are not welcome. This be'eth YouTube, not MeanJerkTube.

Behold! These be'eth the rules of YouTube and the rules be'eth good and right. Learn them well, my sweet child of the Interwebs.

THE COMPLETE TIMELINE OF DAN & PHIL

Recounting the history of YouTube's best double act.

27TH MARCH 2006
PHIL LESTER POSTED HIS FIRST VIDEO

The video was called 'Phil's Video Blog'. Phil was 19 at the time.

25TH OCTOBER 2009
DAN AND PHIL RELEASE THEIR FIRST COLLAB VID

It was called 'phil is not on fire' and started an annual tradition of the pair making a video together (now also known as PINOF).

25TH DECEMBER 2011
THE PAIR HOST A RADIO 1 CHRISTMAS SHOW

Merry Christmas, Phandom!

2006   **2009**   **2010**   **2011**

16TH OCTOBER 2009
DAN HOWELL UPLOADS HIS FIRST VIDEO

It was called 'Hello Internet', but you already knew that, didn't you?

DAN GOES TO MANCHESTER UNIVERSITY TO STUDY LAW

He eventually dropped out to focus on vlogging full time.

10TH AUGUST 2011
DAN MOVES IN WITH PHIL

They lived together in Manchester.

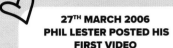
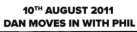

13TH JANUARY 2013
THEIR FIRST WEEKLY RADIO SHOW IS BROADCAST

It's the start of something beautiful.

12TH SEPTEMBER 2014
THEY START THEIR OWN GAMING CHANNEL

They called it DanAndPhilGAMES.

OCTOBER 2015
THEY RELEASE THE AMAZING BOOK IS NOT ON FIRE

And went on a sold-out tour to promote it!

2013　　**2014**　　**2015**　　**2016**　　**NOW!**

4TH FEBRUARY 2013
DAN REACHES 1 MILLION SUBSCRIBERS

 Phil Lester ✔
@AmazingPhil　　　　　　　👤 Follow　∨

"CONGRATULATIONS
@danisnotonfire for 1 MIILLION SUBSCRIBERS!!! :D"
@AmazingPhil/Twitter

Woohoo!

6TH JULY 2013
PHIL REACHES
1 MILLION SUBSCRIBERS

 Phil Lester ✔
@AmazingPhil　　　　　　👤 Follow　∨

"1 MILLION SUBSCRIBERS!!!! :D Woah
thank you so much guys! Can't believe
it. Best 7 years ever! ^__^ <3"
@AmazingPhil/Twitter

Best. Seven. Years. Ever.

29TH NOVEMBER 2016
DAN AND PHIL RELEASE PINOF8

Eight glorious years, already?

HERE'S TO MANY MORE
YEARS OF DAN AND PHIL!

IF YOUR PARENT IS BAFFLED BY YOUR LOVE OF YOUTUBE, JUST USE THIS HANDY GUIDE!

It can be hard to explain the wonderful world of YouTube to your mother, father or other variation of loved one. Use these conversation topics to fully explain what can be, understandably, a pretty confusing world to parents and newcomers alike.

WHAT EXACTLY IS A YOUTUBER?

A YouTuber is anyone who makes videos and puts them on youtube.com specifically for the purpose of entertaining or informing others. There is no specific criteria that makes up a 'YouTuber' and they can span from comedians to musicians to 'vloggers' (we'll get back to them later). One of the appeals of being a YouTuber is the lack of barriers to entry, at least compared to being on TV or in movies.

WHAT IS A VLOGGER THEN?

'Vlogger' is a relatively broad term given to any YouTuber whose main activity is talking directly to the audience. This might be for the sake of comedy, to tell stories, to give advice – but the main appeal is connection. It's like having an Internet best friend. Many of them are charismatic, interesting people that you simply have a fun time listening to. There's nothing in particular that you need to 'get' about it, it's just about simple person-to-person connection.

BUT WHAT DO THEY ACTUALLY DO?

Ah, the age-old question. This is something that confuses people of all ages. It's understandable to watch some YouTubers (particularly vloggers) and to think that they don't seem to be doing very much. But it actually takes a lot of effort to make these videos appear so effortless. Ultimately they may not be displaying a certain talent or skill – they are being generally engaging, in the manner of a talk show host. YouTubers vary, but the key thing to remember is that it's all personality driven. It's not all ego-driven, though. Most YouTubers use their platform to promote healthy ideas like body-positivity, acceptance of others and the understanding of mental health issues.

WHY DO THEY DO IT? DO THEY MAKE MONEY?

Any good YouTuber is making videos because they're passionate about it, but it's also true that these days YouTubers can build a very, very lucrative career out of their videos, with the top YouTubers earning millions every year. That doesn't mean that vloggers should expect to instantly make millions – YouTube is no different to any other form of entertainment business: only some make it to the top. But hey, if someone you know is passionate about YouTubing as a hobby, it's definitely something to encourage, if only for the off-chance that they may end up drowning in $$$.

IS YOUTUBE A SAFE SPACE FOR A YOUNG PERSON?

This is a difficult question to answer because YouTube, like most of the Internet, is a wide-open space. Just as in the real world, there are nice people and mean people. A good thing about YouTube is that it is not as personal or involved as other social media sites like Facebook or Twitter. Interaction is restricted to merely comments on videos – so no one is going to get hold of personal information. Comment sections on random videos are infamously something of a rodeo – it's all just a random, nonsensical mess. But the nice thing about YouTubers (with very few exceptions) is that they tend to have very healthy, positive communities surrounding them. These 'fandoms' (collective noun for a group of fans) are honestly a sort of beacon of light in an otherwise relatively gloomy place (the Internet).

Comment sections on videos posted by popular users tend to be far, far more civil than other videos and they also tend to drift towards self-policing – wherein commenters who are nasty will be driven away by others looking for a more positive experience.

'I'VE HEARD TERRIBLE THINGS ABOUT X YOUTUBER'

Sadly, with the global nature of YouTube and with the number of people finding fame on YouTube growing exponentially year on year, there are occasions where people become famous who later turn out to be unsavoury, or even (allegedly) criminal. Some recent notable examples of YouTubers who have had serious accusations levelled against them are Sam Pepper and Toby Turner. The good news is that: first, these problems are almost always in their private lives and secondly, the YouTube community is very swift and very forceful with shunning those who are revealed to be unpleasant. Mainstream YouTube culture simply doesn't tolerate nasty people. If someone is revealed to be problematic, their career basically ends there and then.

THE BOTTOM LINE

Ultimately it's very harmless. Of all the things for a person to be interested in, YouTube is a pretty good one. It's friendly, it's low-energy and, unless you buy a lot of merchandise (which will be up to you), it's completely free. The fans of YouTubers are no different to fans of bands. Being obsessed with Dan and Phil is no different to Beatlemania. As always, it pays to keep an eye on a young person who spends a lot of time online, as you never know what might happen, but when it comes to YouTube, you can rest assured that it's a fun, healthy and positive area to be interested in.

QUIZ: HOW WELL DO YOU REMEMBER YOUTUBE IN 2008?

"THE LINKS ARE IN THE SIDEBAR..."

We're dialling the Wayback Machine aaalll the way back to the time of YouTube dinosaurs – 2008. Answer the questions to see how well you remember YouTube of yesteryear.

1 Which legendary web series came to an end?

A
Red vs. Blue

B
lonelygirl15

C
The Guild

2 Which of these was NOT a real "FiveAwesome..." collab channel?

A
Gangs

B
Girls

C
Goats

3 What was the name of the first major YouTube gathering?

A
Summer in the City

B
VidCon

C
888

4 Who had more subscribers – Dan or Phil?

A
Dan

B
Phil

Turn to page 93
for the answers!

5 What was the ALL-TIME most viewed video?

A Chocolate Rain

B Evolution of Dance

C Sneezing Panda

6 What HUGE feature did YouTube introduce to its creators?

100K SUBS!

A The Partner Program

B 4K video

C Gold/Silver Play Buttons

7 Name the comedy trio who had YouTube hits such as 'I'm On A Boat' and 'Jack Sparrow'.

A thelonelyisland

B Smosh

C CollegeHumor

8 What MASSIVE subscriber milestone did Charlie McDonnell reach?

A 1,000

B 1,000,000

C 100,000

HERE'S WHY 2017 IS YOUTUBE'S MOST DIVERSE YEAR EVER

With the rise of #YouTubeBlack and a much more diverse ad campaign in 2016, YouTube's move to recognise its minority creators can only improve.

The last year or so has been difficult for YouTube; with issues surrounding drops in views and subscribers, as well as the questionable system for their trending feed which has left creators worried about their future plans. But one thing we can definitely credit YouTube for in their work over the past year, is a new focus on who becomes the face of YouTube; specifically, featuring a much more diverse range of creators wherever they can.

IT BEGAN AT THE END OF BLACK HISTORY MONTH

YouTube's home-built channel YouTube Spotlight shared a video titled 'Keep Making History' on 1st March 2016. The focus was on some of the site's biggest and best black creators, in all their wide range of video styles; and ringing out February's Black History Month, it was a powerful tribute to the future of YouTube and diversity.

Since then, Spotlight has been increasingly rolling out video content that promotes a diverse range of voices amongst the creator community; gender equality, racial stigma and sexual/gender identity have been enormously featured at the forefront of the site, by way of their own channel.

THEN THERE WAS #YouTubeBlack

But YouTube's fight for diversity isn't all a big show; they're taking steps behind the scenes too. Over 2016 YouTube hosted at least three separate events dubbed #YouTubeBlack: two summits in New York and one panel discussion in London.

At each event there was ample discussion on how to promote diversity on the site, as well as creators' influence on how to address racial stigma and political discourse in their videos. More than anything, it was a great chance for black creators to network and uplift each other.

YouTube are regularly hosting similar events at their Spaces across the world. Panels, screenings and workshops with a focus on marginalised identities have become a mainstay in several of their global headquarters.

DIVERSITY WAS ALSO AT THE FRONT OF THEIR ADVERTISING

YouTube's #MadeForYou campaign kicked off at the tail end of 2016; but the most refreshing part of all the posters and pre-roll ads that we saw between November and December was that not every single face was white.

In the past, YouTube have taken flak for the mistake of not diversifying the creators they used for promotion, and they have clearly learned. In all the work they did with their roster of creators in this campaign, there was a conscious effort to be as inclusive and representative as possible.

SO WHY IS 2017 BETTER?

Well for one thing, it has to be. As the world's politics are seemingly turned upside-down, it's up to the social media directive to ensure that a diverse range of voices remain at the forefront of the discussion. Fear and hatred cannot be allowed to dominate the Internet any more than it already has, and the ones holding the keys have to be more conscious of their efforts.

Oona King ✓
@Oona_King   👤 Follow ⌄

"So excited to join @YouTube as Global director [of] diversity [and] marketing. Anyone in broadcasting knows what a great opportunity it is #dreamjob"
@Oona_King/Twitter

Luckily, YouTube has a plan in the form of Oona King. Formerly a Labour politician, Baroness King (yep, she's in the House Of Lords) was hired in the middle of 2016 as YouTube's official global director of diversity, after working in a similar role for Channel 4. King's roots as

Kyle Jones
@OhLookItsAKyle   👤 Follow

"Diversity on YouTube panel was so strong, definitely check it out as soon as it's online, everyone was so great"
@OhLookItsAKyle/Twitter

a mixed-race Jewish African American have helped refine her views and work in social justice; and makes her more than a perfect fit for the role.

And it's not just YouTube putting in the work; the community itself is making a conscious effort to be more inclusive in who they collaborate with and learn from. Almost every major YouTube community event in 2016 made a stronger effort to increase diversity in their attendees and their content.

There's no denying there is still a lot of work to be done; and in an increasingly difficult social climate, what's left to be done will not be easy. But with the right support from major platforms like YouTube working together with the community, we can celebrate the beauty of its diversity loudly and proudly.

FANCY DRESS COSTUMES ONLY TRUE YOUTUBE FANS WOULD EVER EVEN ATTEMPT

You ready to get real?

From vloggers to viral videos and beloved videogame characters, there's a lot of fancy dress inspo to be found from all of your favourite corners of YouTube. Fans of Miranda Sings, Dil Howter and, er, that girl who crashed her dad's BBC interview, these dress-up ideas will make sure you stay panic-free when your best mate's cousin's sister's fancy dress party invite arrives in your inbox. (Or, you know, for your average Friday night at home. Whatever floats your boat, we ain't here to judge).

1. MIRANDA SINGS

Miranda's style is simple but iconic; even just the red pants and the heavy lipstick will be enough to convince everyone of your costume. But if you want to go all-out, here is the ultimate costume kit:

- "Haters Back Off" sweatpants
- Pink Crocs
- Red lipstick (lots)
- Oversized leopard print shirt

2. DIL HOWLTER

The Sims-based lovechild of Dan & Phil had a pretty signature look from the day of his creation; thanks to the Internet and some dedicated Phangirls, you can recreate it to the letter! You will need:

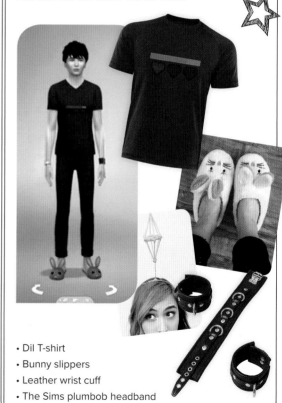

- Dil T-shirt
- Bunny slippers
- Leather wrist cuff
- The Sims plumbob headband

3. PIZZA RAT

This season's most relatable viral sensation will probably already have hundreds of costumes dedicated to it – but ours is all about the fully authentic New Yorker experience. Here's how to transform yourself into the perfect Pizza Rat this Halloween:

- Rat costume
- Large slice of New York-Style pizza
- Dirt (optional)
- New York Subway pass

4. HANNAH HART (CARROT ONESIE MODE)

Carrot onesie, carrot carrot onesie, carrot onesie, carrot carrot onesie:

- Carrot onesie
- That's it
- No "off button"

5. STEPHANO (PEWDIEPIE'S AMNESIA STATUE)

There's already been some incredible cosplay of Pewds' trusty spiritual guide from his Amnesia series (believe me, we Googled it), but here's how you can affordably replicate a real-life edition of the little golden statue:

- Gold biblical shepherd costume
- Gold pointed shoes
- Wooden scimitar
- Metallic gold body paint

6. MARION KELLY (THAT GIRL WHO CRASHED HER DAD'S BBC INTERVIEW)

Marion Kelly aka the dancing kid that nearly ruined her dad's life on live TV is first and foremost one of the most iconic people to ever bless YouTube, but secondly is a really classic dresser. Meaning it's easy to steal her look. Keep doing what you do, Marion:

- Yellow jumper
- Glasses: Steal your mum's, grandma's or mate's for the night.
- Pigtails
- Angry Dad: optional

WHAT SHOULD YOU CALL YOUR VLOG CHANNEL?

YOU'RE THINKING OF STARTING A VLOGGING CHANNEL — BUT WHAT WILL YOU CALL IT? WELL, USING OUR HANDY CHANNEL NAME GENERATOR YOU CAN FIND OUT RIGHT NOW!

Naming a channel is hard, but thankfully we've created a totally scientific way to find out the perfect name for you. Follow steps 1, 2 and 3 below and see what yours should be. We can't wait to subscribe!

1. YOUR BIRTH MONTH

JANUARY/JUNE	FEBRUARY/AUGUST	MARCH/SEPTEMBER
THE	**[YOUR 1ST NAME]'S**	**IT'S THE**
APRIL/OCTOBER	MAY/NOVEMBER	JULY/DECEMBER
[NO 1ST WORD]	**MY**	**THAT**

2. FIRST LETTER OF YOUR FIRST NAME

A - ONE N' ONLY	G - VLOG	M - CHAT	S - LAME	Y - NICE
B - CHATTING	H - HALF ASLEEP	N - ONLY	T - PAL	Z - YAP
C - TALKING	I - FOOD ADDICT	O - CONVO	U - CHILL	
D - CHATTIN'	J - CHILL	P - SLEEPY	V - ONLY	
E - VLOG	K - TALK	Q - VIDEO	W - BUDDY	
F - TALKING	L - CHATTING	R - FRIEND	X - FREN	

3. FIRST LETTER OF YOUR LAST NAME

A - CLUBHOUSE	G - LIFE	M - PALACE	S - BOSS	Y - WIZARD
B - KING	H - ZONE	N - HOUSE	T - TIME	Z - BOI
C - DON	I - BOSS	O - HAUS	U - KING	
D - CLUB	J - CREW	P - TIME	V - ZONE	
E - FAMILY	K - EXPERT	Q - GENIUS	W - CHANNEL	
F - CHANNEL	L - 4EVA	R - TIME	X - GANG	

QUIZ: ARE YOU AN INTROVERT, AN EXTROVERT – OR LILLY SINGH?

There are three types of people in this crazy world of ours and you without doubt can be categorised as one of them. Outgoing extroverts, shy introverts... or, er, Canadian YouTube star Lilly Singh. Simply answer the questions below and add up your score to find out where you fall.

1 Where is your favourite place to hang out?

A At a party

B Lilly Singh's house (which I just call 'my house')

C At home

2 How do you feel about public speaking?

A It's fine

B I went on a tour called 'A Trip to Unicorn Island'

C HATE IT

3 How smooth are you?

A AS SILK BABY!

B I'm also known as IISuperwomanII

C AS A CACTUS BABY!

4 What do you look for in a romantic partner?

A Someone to share adventures with

B Someone to discuss unicorns with

C Someone supportive

5 Pick a season:

A Summer

B Spring

C Winter

6 What do you say when people tell you to "just stop being shy"?

A "Oh great thanks I will"

B "I am from Toronto"

C "Oh great thanks I will" (sarcastically)

7 How loud are you?

A Pretty loud

B I have a degree in psychology

C Kinda quiet

8 Socialising is:

A The best

B My Name is Lilly

C Tiring

9 Pick an object:

A A key

B An amulet

C A candlestick

Mostly As...
You are an extrovert
You love to socialise and p-a-r-t-y!

Mostly Bs...
You are Lilly Singh
OMG! Hi Lilly! We're huge fans!

Mostly Cs...
You are an introvert
Remember, the quietest minds often have the loudest thoughts.

SIX LESSONS I LEARNT ABOUT BEING A YOUTUBER AT VIDCON

From friendship, professionalism, and the quest for fame, Liam Dryden shares what he learnt at VidCon.

Taking place in California every summer since 2009, John and Hank Green's signature online video convention has become an annual marker for who's big on YouTube right now, what the Next Big Thing might be – and on a personal level, what stage one's career is at. This was my sixth VidCon in a row, and after a hiatus from YouTube, was the first one at which I wasn't required to speak at any panels. I saw this year as a good opportunity for networking, self-reflection, and above all, learning where to go next. So from a mixture of panels, meetings, parties, and one amazing interview, here's everything I learned at VidCon about what it means to be a YouTuber these days.

1. SURROUND YOURSELF WITH PEOPLE WHO GENUINELY SUPPORT YOU

In an impassioned speech at the VidCon Creator Keynote, storyteller and sketch genius Olan Rogers shared what keeps him going on YouTube, and subsequently what has made him great: the love and support of a team of friends.

"It is so easy to have negative people affect you, while being a creator," admits Olan. "I've seen so many YouTube friendships disintegrate because the wrong people are involved with your creating."

"Surround yourself with people that are positive, uplift you, and want you to succeed; I guarantee you that you can do freakin' anything." (VidCon/YouTube)

I talked to many people over the weekend about the level of competition amongst YouTubers, as well as the ideas of "strategic collaboration" and those who cling to rising creators to grow their own audience. Most

admitted they were sick of the blatant social climbing and career-driven friendships within the community; especially those that resulted in disingenuous people becoming successful.

As YouTube reaches new heights, and would-be Internet stars compete for the attention of their audiences, a common train of thought amongst genuine creators seemed to be that healthy relationships and great content are much more rewarding goals than a million of someone else's subscribers.

2. YOUTUBE MIGHT NOT BE THE PLATFORM FOR YOU, AND THAT'S OKAY

At the same Creator Keynote where Olan expressed his secret to success on YouTube, extreme sports videographer Devin Graham burst onstage with a plethora of advice; including an interesting tidbit about "one of [his] favourite social media people", video SFX wizard FinalCutKing.

Zach King had apparently started uploading his video-based trickery to YouTube, where it wasn't having great reach. But after swapping out YouTube for Vine and Instagram as his primary hubs for content, King now boasts over 1.3 billion Vine loops, and 14 million Instagram followers.

Devin's advice might be a controversial

statement to make at a convention that primarily celebrates YouTube and YouTubers, but this is the reality of the future of online video. With Instagram, and even Facebook; there are several more competitors to YouTube than there have been in previous years, and each has its own unique audience and identifiers that might prove themselves a more successful platform for you. If you find you haven't had much success with YouTube, it's not an admission of defeat to try and expand your audience with a different platform.

3. CREATORS NEED TO UNIONISE

Shady multi-channel networks. Brand deals that offer less than a standard freelance rate. YouTubers that are willing to work "for exposure", thus making it harder for the ones that need to earn. These are just a few of the ways in which creators struggle to grow or support themselves as "YouTuber" becomes less of a sensational title and more of just a career path (implications of that to be discussed over the page).

Fortunately, VidCon head honcho and all-round entrepreneur Hank Green knows this more than anybody – and has the means to do something about it.

Hank's new project, the Internet Creators Guild, was announced a week before VidCon; but in his final speech at the event, Hank officially launched the project – revealing that creators could finally sign up to join a unionised collective and support network of people who earn a living making things online.

Again, as the YouTube sphere grows beyond anyone's comprehension, it's important now more than ever for creators to agree on how our business is conducted. This initiative, as long as enough creators are willing to either get in line or join a similar outfit, will hopefully revolutionise the way that YouTube creators are treated; not just in their industry, but also in the media, in the respect and security they are afforded, and in the legitimisation of online video as its own art form.

4. STAY HUMBLE, AND STAY GENUINE

During VidCon, I had the pleasure of meeting and interviewing one of the most exciting creators on the Internet right now – Vine darling and YouTube newcomer Thomas Sanders, attending the event for the first time. The day before our interview, I thanked him for all the love he's been giving wetheunicorns.com recently. His response was to hug me, and admit that our articles made him feel incredibly included within the YouTube community.

Even off-camera, Thomas retains his infectious positivity; and thanks to this genuine trait, our conversations over the next couple of days continued to be nothing but pleasant. Overall, his humble nature and his earnestness were far more refreshing than some of the griping I had admittedly shared with other creators this weekend.

Complaints from fellow YouTubers about not →

being paid enough for a brand deal, or whether or not they deserved an invite to all of VidCon's parties had taken over more of my event than I had realised – and in a 30-minute conversation with one of social media's fastest-rising stars, I was quickly reminded that entitlement is one of the most debilitating qualities that sadly pervades the YouTube community.

Thomas and others like him are proof that positivity as a part of your online brand will get you far; but genuine positivity and humbleness will keep you there.

5. NOT EVERYONE WILL EVER KNOW YOU – AND YOU WON'T EVER KNOW EVERYONE

Being a guest of VidCon usually means having a couple of extra privileges; including access to a few areas that are off-limits to other attendees. But as I hung out with friends in backstage areas and creator lounges this year, I started to notice that the familiar faces are becoming more and more outweighed by strangers – many of whom I would later learn have audiences of 3-5 million subscribers and above.

As I keep reiterating: YouTube is big now. Like, impossibly big. There are literally hundreds of thousands of young people all vying for YouTube stardom. As much as we'd love to believe our little corner of #TeamInternet is niche, the truth is it's still a pretty big corner.

It ties back into the "stay humble" lesson, but if your goal in becoming a successful YouTuber is to be known and loved by everyone, prepare for disappointment. But at the same time, chances are you won't always know everyone around you either. So it's okay! Apparently the 'Star Wars' cast didn't recognise Jennifer Lawrence one time and she made a fool of herself. So it's not just us.

6. "YOUTUBER" IS A BAD JOB TITLE

One of the most intriguing panels I attended was "Is There Anything New To Watch?", moderated

by Jack Howard, and featuring Bertie Gilbert, Savannah Brown, Will Darbyshire and Hannah Witton. The panel was founded on the basis of a discussion sparked by Jack, on the idea that the "mainstream model" of content has become oversaturated to the point where it's hard to find anything new or different.

During the panel, someone brought up that they were fairly uncomfortable with the catchall term of "YouTuber" to define their work. Which is fair, as every panellist creates completely different types of content – from short films, to slam poetry, to sex education. These are strands of video types that are not well represented under the umbrella term of "YouTuber", and most prefer to define themselves otherwise.

People that look up to "YouTubers" or have dreams of becoming a "professional YouTuber" are often of the belief that this title is a self-sustaining path to stardom; that it doesn't matter what you are uploading, as long as you're a YouTuber, you have the right to succeed. But it is easy to forget that YouTube is a platform, rather than a profession – and without a clear style of content that is true to one's self, it is incredibly hard to break the mould and succeed on the site.

There was a lot more to learn at this year's VidCon – and so much of it I missed by attending other things. But as a creator in need of a serious reboot, the chance to watch from the side-lines on how other creators are managing their own worlds taught me the most obvious lesson of them all: to do well on YouTube, Instagram or any other platform of your choosing, you just have to do you.

QUIZ: WHAT PERCENTAGE DAN HOWELL ARE YOU?

HOW MUCH HOWELL IS THERE IN YOUR SOUL?

Simply answer the questions below and then add up your score. We think you'll be surprised at the results.

1 How do you like your memes?

A Family friendly
B I loathe memes
C DANK AF
D Relatively dank
E DANK

2 Favourite lunar state:

A Mooning
B Eclipse
C Exploded
D Full Moon
E Half Moon

3 Cry or craft?

A Cry
B Craft

4 Pick a Disney film:

A 'Big Hero 6'
B 'Cars'
C 'The Fox & The Hound'
D 'The Lion King'
E 'Finding Nemo'

5 Favourite kind of end screen dance?

A The Robot
B The Cha Cha Slide
C Alluring
D Suggestive
E Sexy

6 Pick a 'Call Of Duty' experience:

A Advanced Warfare (Normal Difficulty)
B World At War (Veteran Difficulty)
C World At War (Zombies)
D Infinite Warfare (Multiplayer)
E Infinite Warfare (Veteran Difficulty)

7 Pick a Muse album:

A 'Drones'
B 'Black Holes and Revelations'
C 'The Resistance'
D 'Origin of Symmetry'
E 'The 2nd Law'

1.	a.+1	b.+0	c.+4	d.+2	e.+3
2.	a.+2	b.+4	c.+0	d.+1	e.+3
3.	a.+0	b.+4			
4.	a.+4	b.+1	c.+0	d.+3	e.+2
5.	a.+1	b.+0	c.+3	d.+1	e.+4
6.	a.+1	b.+4	c.+3	d.+1	e.+0
7.	a.+0	b.+3	c.+2	d.+4	e.+1

Use this grid to add up your score.

0-5...
You are 0% Dan Howell, and we're so sorry to break the bad news.

6-10...
You are 25% Dan Howell, which is like a leg or something.

11-17...
You are 50% Dan Howell, but you can decide if it's your top or bottom half...

18-25...
You are 75% Dan Howell, because no one can truly be as perfect as he is.

26+
You are 100% Dan Howell. In fact, aren't you just Dan? No one else could have scored so well on this quiz unless they were the real thing...

23

WHY IS TRADITIONAL MEDIA STILL OBSESSED WITH YOUTUBERS' MONEY?

We're going to reveal some crazy insider info about the YouTube world; we are dropping some knowledge that might rock you and the entire media industry to its core, and nobody can stop us. Are you ready? Make sure you're sitting down for this. It's a major scoop too, so get a pen ready. Through a mixture of advertising revenue, paid endorsements and merchandising, some YouTubers can get paid for their videos. I know, mind-blowing.

Ever since Google launched the Partner Program in 2008, money has been a pretty prominent concept in the world of YouTube. Some creators might earn a few hundred dollars of ad revenue a year, as a perk for doing something they enjoy; while others are literal millionaires who, through viral success, brand deals and merchandise, have become household brand names.

Of course, everyone already knows all of this. It's not news. YouTubers have become a lot more transparent about the way the money rolls in, to the point where even casual viewers are unfazed.

And yet, every time an event happens within the YouTube community that's large enough to break beyond the bubble of social media and grab the attention of mainstream news outlets, a dozen traditional publications will spend half

the story prattling on about "these millennial celebs you've never heard of", make fun of their teenage audiences, and then obsess about their money.

Gaming giant PewDiePie was aggressively placed under the world news' microscope in 2015, after it was revealed that he earned over $7 million in 2014. The viral nature of this story was so intense that Felix had to address it on his channel, talking about his rapid rise to fame, the commercial success that came with it, and other people's apparent obsession with his bank statement.

The fallout from this discussion apparently had some staying power, as it was still on the minds of many major news outlets over a month later. Summer in the City 2016, the UK's largest YouTuber event, was held in August

in London's ExCeL centre. With a sold-out capacity of 10,000, the scale and nature of the event caught the eye of traditional media outlets like ITV, Sky News and the BBC; the latter of which interviewed organiser Tom Burns and guest creator TomSka. The segment is sadly no longer available, but according to the interviewees, the lengthy answers they gave the Beeb were... slightly less represented in the final result.

Here was an opportunity for a major TV news outlet to highlight literally any other facet of the event – the packed main stage for unknown acts, the lengthy panels on industry and community (of which there were four per hour), or even the crowds of hyperactive fans bonding over a shared love of a creator in the meet and greet lines. But nah, let's remind the world that there's profit in this for some reason.

No other professional in any field has to repeatedly justify their earnings in this way; not even others who work in the public eye. Actors, pop stars, footballers and even reality TV personalities with fanbases half as engaged as one of the top subscribed YouTube channels can earn three times as much, and somehow it doesn't warrant a headline. And yet a decade after the site's launch, print media is still insistent on patronising creators, their fans and even their own readership by harping on about how "there's gold in that there newfangled YouTube thing".

It's boring, it's antiquated, in some cases it's a straight-up invasion of privacy – in case you forgot, the Daily Mail published (since removed) photos of the inside, outside and location of Zoë and Alfie's new home in Brighton, just because the story of a YouTuber buying a

£1 million house was just too juicy to afford them any privacy – but more than anything, it's just not news.

There have been some ham-fisted thoughtpiece-y attempts to spin the money discussion into the idea that these creators are bad role models for kids, because "something something YouTube ads for sweets something something". But if young people's role models are composed of young entrepreneurs earning their millions armed with a video camera and an innate ability to genuinely connect with people, then a medium that attempts to derail that genuineness with scare tactics should feel very, very threatened.

The need to define everything new and strange by the money that surrounds it is an archaic concept that print media clings to – it'll be fun to see how long that sinking ship stays afloat.

LOOKING TO GET IN SHAPE? HERE IS THE PERFECT FITNESS PLAN TO MATCH SOME OF YOUR FAVOURITE TYPES OF YOUTUBE VIDEOS.

Whether it's 'New Year, New You', or you just fancy getting a little more in shape, we all promise ourselves we're going to stick to a new regimen. But coming up with fitness plans is hard, right? Well don't worry; once again, we've got you covered with another YouTube-related solution to something we are definitely not experts in. So strap into your gym shorts and follow the instructions below for a serious YouTube workout.

HOW DO THEY WORK?
For everything you see or hear in each of these video themes, you do the little bit of workout recommended.

WILL THIS GIVE ME A KILLER BOD?
Maybe not by itself, but consider this a primer for getting into the habit of exercising. You never know; associating it with your favourite YouTubers might help you love the routine.

WHY WOULD YOU MAKE ME EXERCISE WHEN ALL I WANT TO DO IS WATCH DODIE?
Hey, we're not the boss of you, this is just a suggestion pal.

VLOGS
For when your YouTube faves are going on for over 10 minutes about a story that definitely really happened (not clickbait)...

EVERY TIME...
THEY CLAP AT THE START OF THE VIDEO:
10 PUSH-UPS

YOU HEAR "SORRY I HAVEN'T UPLOADED IN A WHILE":
10 PUSH-UPS

THE VIDEO IS #SPON:
5 LUNGES

THEY ASK YOU TO CLICK "LIKE" BEFORE THEY DO ANYTHING ELSE:
5 JUMPING JACKS

YOU LAUGH OUT LOUD: 10 SQUATS

THEY ASK YOU TO "BELL THEM"/"TURN ON NOTIFICATIONS FOR THEIR UPLOADS":
10 LUNGES

COLLABS

Think you've seen this challenge being done before? Or looking for something to do while PINOF is on in the background? Time to sweat! Invite a workout buddy to maximise the experience.

EVERY TIME...

YOU HEAR "HEY GUYS":
10 JUMPING JACKS

YOU SEE A DELIBERATE BLOOPER:
5 LUNGES

YOU HEAR THE WORD "CHALLENGE":
10 PUSH-UPS

SOMEONE LAUGHS TOO LOUD:
5 CRUNCHES

THEY REFERENCE AN OLD VIDEO:
5 SQUATS

THEY ASK YOU TO SUBSCRIBE TO THEIR FRIEND:
10 JUMPING JACKS

BONUS: IF YOU'RE ALREADY SUBSCRIBED:
10 PUSH-UPS

MORNING/"GET READY WITH ME" ROUTINES

Jealous of people that have time to go to the gym in the morning? Put one of these videos on and pretend you just got up!

EVERY TIME...

THEY'RE PRETENDING TO BE ASLEEP:
10 CRUNCHES

THEY MAKE A HOT BEVERAGE:
5 PUSH-UPS

THEY SAY THEY CAN'T DO ANYTHING WITHOUT HAVING SAID BEVERAGE:
5 JUMPING JACKS

BREAKFAST LOOKS TOO COMPLICATED TO MAKE:
5 SQUATS

A BRAND IS MENTIONED:
5 LUNGES

THEY ACCOMPLISH EVERYTHING BEFORE 8AM:
10 CRUNCHES

BONUS: IF YOU EVER THINK "GOALS":
10 PUSH-UPS

BINGO! YOUTUBE DRAMA EDITION

OMG!

Fed up of your favourite YouTubers subtweeting each other? Turn it into a game!

YouTube is a very dramatic place. With so many huge personalities, each with their own army of devoted fans, it's a wonder we haven't had a nuclear apocalypse yet. Although that might be down to the fact that most of the beef takes the form of subtweets and vague commentary instead of massive battles. We've started to notice patterns every time drama kicks off, so we put together a little game. Yep, it's Bingo.

How to play:
the boring bit zzzzz

- Check off a box whenever you see/hear the relevant thing happen.
- Continue as necessary until you check off five boxes in a row: horizontal, vertical and diagonal all apply.
- The FREE SPACE allows you to complete a row that passes through the middle for free.
- HARD MODE: Go for a Full House (checking off every box).

"STOP SPREADING NEGATIVITY!"	ACCUSATIONS OF JEALOUSY	SUBTWEET ABOUT WISHING PEOPLE WOULD BE MORE DIRECT	"WHAT'S HAPPENING?" "DM'D YOU X"	PITHY METAPHOR ABOUT FLOWERS OR CANDLES
A NEW "YOUTUBE HAS CHANGED" VLOG WITHIN A DAY	THE WORD "BEEF" APPEARS IN ANY CONTEXT	PHANDOM GETS INVOLVED SOMEHOW	SEMI-RELATED DEBATE ARTICLE FROM WE THE UNICORNS	FAN REPLIES TO BASIC SUBTWEET WITH "YASS DRAG THEM"
UNINVOLVED PERSON STARTS BLATANTLY SOCIAL CLIMBING	SOMEONE POSTS THAT GIF OF TROY WITH THE PIZZA FROM 'COMMUNITY'	FREE SPACE!	PERSON INVOLVED STARTS TWEETING ABOUT HOW GREAT THEIR DAY IS GOING	300 TWEETS ASKING WHAT'S GOING ON
".@"	FANS TURN INTO INVESTIGATIVE JOURNALISTS	SOMEONE LITERALLY USES THE HASHTAG #SUBTWEET	"STEPPING AWAY FROM SOCIAL MEDIA FOR A WHILE GUYS XX"	" 🙊 "
PERSON INVOLVED GETS CAUGHT LIKING SHADY TWEETS	THE ARGUMENT HAPPENS LITERALLY EVERYWHERE BUT YOUTUBE	"ANYWAY ENOUGH OF THAT, WHO'S EXCITED FOR MY NEW VIDEO?"	SOMEONE TALKS ABOUT BEING "ABOVE IT ALL" INSTEAD OF JUST STAYING QUIET	BEYONCÉ OR DRAG RACE GIF IS USED IN AN "I DON'T CARE" CAPACITY

QUIZ: DO YOU KNOW THESE YOUTUBERS' REAL NAMES?

YouTubers, much like superheroes, will often be known by nicknames (usernames really) – and often these nicknames may become more well-known then their real name, leading to situations like when newspapers refer to Zoë as 'Zoella Sugg' (yes that actually happens). As true YouTube fans, your test, whether you choose to accept it or not, is to show just how well you know the birth names of some of your favourite online Fun People. Let's play!

Turn to page 93 for the answers!

JACKSEPTICEYE

GRAV3YARDGIRL

POINTLESSBLOG

DANISNOTONFIRE

LOHANTHONY

WHEEZYWAITER

SEANANNERS

JENNAMARBLES

PSYCHOSOPRANO

THE 50 BEST YOUTUBE VIDEOS OF ALL TIME

DID YOUR YOUTUBER FAVE MAKE THE LIST?

Music fans and film fans are always ranking their favourite songs and movies. So why can't YouTube fans get in on the fun?

To start, here is a list of the 50 greatest YouTube videos of all time... according to us. Tick off the videos you've seen, and add up your score. Make sure to load up YouTube and watch any you haven't seen (we promise you won't be disappointed). And if your favourite didn't make the list, then share the awesomeness with us @wetheunicorns.

50. RICKROLL'D (COTTER548)

Listen, we all know what this video is, there's no need to linger on it too long – but – as irritating as this video has been for longer than we all care to remember, there's no denying that it has a special place in the online history books.

49. WELCOME TO FANDOM SCHOOL (COLLISCOOL)

She may be relatively new on the YouTube scene but Coll *is* cool and has earned a place on our list. As this YouTube star continues to ascend, don't be surprised if she creates a video that appears further along in the list. In the meantime, watch her incredible parody of fandoms.

48. HOWTOBASIC

If you haven't experienced the magic(?) of How To Basic we don't want to ruin things for you, so you should stop reading and go watch a video. Fans of this faceless fiend will understand why we think he's one of the most unique YouTubers to ever arrive on the scene.

47. "CHOCOLATE RAIN" ORIGINAL SONG (TAY ZONDAY)

Remember this silly song? Well we recently Googled the lyrics and it turns out the song is actually very explicitly and poignantly about racism – so there's that. It's a catchy-as-hell song for the ages and yeah, turns out it's got a meaning behind it too. Good stuff.

46. EVOLUTION OF DANCE (JUDSON LAIPPLY)

This video was also one of the first viral videos that revolved around someone actively doing something, rather than just capturing something weird on camera. It was someone who had created what we now all delightfully refer to as 'content'.

45. CHARLIE BIT MY FINGER - AGAIN! (HDCYT)

Okay, look – we know that everyone is sick of this video, but it was once the most viewed video of all time and it was one of the very first truly viral videos, so it deserves a place here for the sake of history.

44. JESUS CHRIST IN RICHMOND PARK (JAGGL113)

FENTON! FENTON! FENTOOOOOON! If you haven't seen this beautiful bit of canine nonsense, change that right now.

43. 99 RED BALLOONS - PLAYED WITH RED BALLOONS (ANDREW HUANG)

It's exactly what it sounds like and it's awesome. 4 million views can't be wrong!

42. HOW ANIMALS EAT THEIR FOOD (MISTER EPIC MANN)

This video is so dumb. So, so dumb – and so good.

41. WE GOT A PUPPY! (TANYA BURR)

Tanya is a treat, puppies are a treat – do we need to say more?

40. POTTER PUPPET PALS: THE MYSTERIOUS TICKING NOISE (NEIL CICIEREGA)

What is that Mysterious Ticking Noise? We'll tell you what it is – it's the sound of an absolutely brilliant YouTube video! It's a testament to how funny this

video is that we can watch it today, over a decade after it was released and still laugh like crazy.

39. SAIL – AWOLNATION (UNOFFICIAL VIDEO) (NANALEW)

This amazing fake video for the song 'Sail' is so iconic that it's still closely associated with the nautical banger to this very day. It's really well shot and very funny – take a look!

38. JACOB (THE FEDORA) VLOG (REGALJOE)

regaljoe is relatively new to the YouTube scene, but he's already making waves with his uniquely hilarious ability to create and inhabit original comedy characters. Jacob is one of his greatest creations and never stops being terrifyingly accurate.

37. BITE ME (FEAT. CRABSTICKZ) (TOMSKA)

Tom and his team make what may well be the most professionally produced comedy sketches on all of YouTube. They are also really, really funny. This video (which features fellow list-member Chris Kendall) is really, really funny. Watch it (because it's funny). →

36. JUST GIRLY THINGS (EMMABLACKERY)

When we reached out to our readers, asking them to suggest their favourite videos of all time, this video popped up time and time again. To be honest with you, we can totally see why: it's a perfect example of Emma's dry yet relatable sense of humour.

35. GRAND THEFT AUTO PACIFIST (GOLDVISION)

GoldVision is one of the best new gaming YouTubers out there. His GTA Pacifist series is a great example of the kind of original angles he takes in his creations. The series follows his adventures as he tries to play GTA Online as a total pacifist. It sounds silly – and it is – but it's also often bizarrely touching.

34. BIKE LANES (CASEYNEISTAT)

Casey is known for his carefully constructed and often thought-provoking videos – and this is no exception. It was one of his first big viral hits (although by no means his last) and boasts the ever-perfect combo of being both hilarious and having a message.

33. WHY CAN'T I BE A DISNEY PRINCESS (ITSWAYPASTMYBEDTIME)

Carrie shows off her signature pipes and cheeky sense of humour in this catchy little number. It's a great example of why she has taken the world of YouTube (and the stage) by storm.

32. SIGNS A GUY DOESN'T LIKE YOU (CONNORFRANTA)

Can't beat a bit of Franta and this uber-popular video will show you exactly why.

31. SHE - ORIGINAL SONG (DODDLEODDLE)

Dodie has tons of awesome videos where she performs unique covers and beautifully-penned original songs. Of all her songs, 'She' may be the one that stands out the most, just in terms of being most able to utterly stun a crowd. It's raw, it's honest and it's sweet.

30. LIVES CHANGED FOREVER! (SACCONEJOLYS)

The Saccone-Jolys have revolutionsied what it means to be a daily vlogger by offering unprecedented access into the day-to-day lives of their family. This video is one of the most magical episodes of their lives that they've ever shared.

29. LET'S TALK ABOUT SEX (TROYE SIVAN)

Troye is now of course most well known for his fantastically successful music career but before he graced the world's arenas he was a YouTuber making videos in his bedroom. Some of his best videos deal with serious, educational topics – like this excellent sex education video.

28. YOU LOOK DISGUSTING (MY PALE SKIN)

"Three months ago, I began posting images of

myself without makeup on social media. The following film contains real comments that were left on images of my face." That's the description under Em Ford's uber-viral video, though no words can really do justice to the effect it has on the viewer. It's an uncomfortable viewing experience, but a necessary one.

27. SOMETHING I WANT YOU TO KNOW (COMING OUT) (INGRID NILSEN)

It took an unbelievable amount of strength for Ingrid to make and release this video revealing the truth about her sexuality. The emotional strain is clear throughout, but she powers through and creates one of the most important videos in the history of YouTube.

26. LET'S PLAY – WWE '13 (ROOSTER TEETH)

The WWE (wrestling) video games have some very in-depth character creators, which allows players to create truly horrifying custom wrestlers. That is precisely what Rooster Teeth did here, with incredible results. This video is too funny.

25. MY DRUNK PUMPKIN (MYHARTO)

Truly you'd be hard pressed to find a better example of what makes 'the trinity' so beloved. This iconic video is pure hilarity – because at the end of the day

there is nothing like watching three very funny best friends getting ludicrously drunk and going off the rails together.

24. SPACE ADVENTURE! (KICKTHEPJ)

PJ is one of the most creative YouTubers working today and this video is a beautiful example of that. He is the king of doing more with less, expertly creating magical visuals using simple homemade sets and effects. It's arts and crafts to the beautiful max.

23. HI, I'M A SLUT: A SLAM POEM (SAVANNAH BROWN)

Savannah's videos don't mess around – and sometimes that's exactly what you want, particularly when you're dealing with the kinds of issues she tends to tackle. This slam poem has been lauded for its frankness, honesty and for Savannah's unapologetic approach to daring to live her life as a woman.

22. FINISHING WITH SPRINKLEOFGLITTER (SPRINKLEOFGLITTER)

This was one of the most important YouTube (and YouTuber) videos ever produced. It was the moment a beloved creator decided to take a risk in order to make their videos more honest and real. It took guts and thankfully, it paid off. →

21. NASH GRIER RANT (RE: WHAT GUYS LOOK FOR IN GIRLS) (THETHIRDPEW)

This video really shows what makes Nathan the YouTube star of tomorrow through it's combination of top notch humour and a legitimate message – yes, he's adeptly roasting Nash and his pals, but he's doing it for a genuinely serious and positive reason. Nice job, Nathan.

20. BOUNCE (FT. TIMOTHY DELAGHETTO) (JUSREIGN)

This video is arguably perfect – and by 'arguably' we mean it is perfect. It's perfect. It's so Zen and peaceful yet so funny. It's a masterpiece.

19. OUIJA BOARD CHALLENGE! (SHANE)

Shane truly has to be praised for his ability to stay both relevant and entertaining despite being one of the oldest YouTubers on the site (in terms of career not age). He's a YouTube veteran and he's still producing the goods. This video is no exception.

18. WHERE MY BAES AT? – ORIGINAL SONG BY MIRANDA SINGS (MIRANDA SINGS)

Miranda is legendary for her world-class singing voice and internationally recognised humility. This is an example of this songstress at her very best.

17. AMAZING YOUTUBER IMPRESSIONS (THATCHERJOE)

Joe Sugg is one of the most popular YouTubers on the ol' YouTubes as well as here at Unicorns – and with good reason. Joe is extremely likeable and always a good laugh. He also has an uncanny ability for impressions, as shown in his YouTuber impression showcase.

16. HAPPY WHEELS – PART 1 (JACKSEPTICEYE)

Jack's Happy Wheels series is arguably what put this cheeky Irish chappy on the map. Viewers fell in love with his high-energy approach to this insane game and the characters he developed as it progressed.

15. AFTER EVER AFTER – DISNEY PARODY (PAINT)

The Unicorns team had the pleasure of watching Jon perform this song live at SITC 2016, and to say that the audience were utterly entranced would be the understatement of the century. Jon is capable of fantastic parody and biting satire, but let's not forget that the dude has also got some crazy-good pipes.

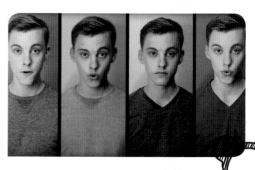

14. WHAT COLOR IS A MIRROR? (VSAUCE)

Vsauce is still the leader of the pack when it comes to info-tainment on YouTube. Michael's videos are meticulously researched, often really funny and have an uncanny ability to leave you feeling shaken up, in the best possible way.

13. WARNING: SCARIEST GAME IN YEARS | FIVE NIGHTS AT FREDDY'S – PART 1 (MARKIPLIER)

Markiplier is one of the most popular YouTubers on our site – you guys just go crazy for him. His Five Nights At Freddy's series is legendary – and this is where it all began.

12. WHISPERING AWKWARD PICKUP LINES (FT. CONNOR FRANTA) (TYLER OAKLEY)

Tyler is hilarious, Connor is always a delight – so the two of them together? It's the recipe for a ludicrously entertaining video!

11. PROVING THE ILLUMINATI IS REAL! (NIGAHIGA)

Ryan Higa has created loads of incredible videos. We were having a hard time choosing, but luckily one of our readers suggested this video and we thought it was a great choice!

10. CHRIOS KENDALLAS | CHRIS KENDALL (CRABSTICKZ)

We are unashamed Chris Kendall fans, so when it came time to pick one video that represents his particular brand of lunacy, it proved pretty hard.

In the end we went with this telenovela because it will make you laugh, cry and applaud – often simultaneously. It is truly a masterpiece.

9. POKEMON IN REAL LIFE! (SMOSH)

Smosh have been on YouTube for a good few years but they're still knocking it outta the park. This classic series is a fantastic example of the kind of magic these two best friends create on an almost daily basis.

8. SUPERMAN WITH A GOPRO (CORRIDOR)

'Superman With A GoPro' is stunning, it's fun, uplifting and it's honestly better than a lot of actual, multi-million dollar superhero films. It's just awesome.

7. DUET WITH MYSELF (CHARLIEISSOCOOLLIKE)

This video may seem unimpressive – but you need to understand, when it was released in 2009, it was genuinely ground breaking. It changed the public perception of what a YouTube video could be – something that Charlie has done since the beginning of his YouTube career and continues to do to this day.

6. DOG OF WISDOM (JOE)

We have been very nice about the previous videos on this list, but none of them hold a candle to this, the greatest YouTube video ever made. →

WE ASKED YOU TO VOTE ONLINE FOR YOUR TOP FIVE VIDEOS OF ALL TIME, AND HERE ARE THE RESULTS:

5. OK GO - HERE IT GOES AGAIN (OKGOVEVO)

Receiving 4% of the votes, it's OKGo, dancing on treadmills!

4. ME AT THE ZOO (JAWED)

With just 5% of the votes, the first YouTube video EVER comes in at number four.

3. CHARLIE THE UNICORN (FILMCOW)

Charlie the grumpy unicorn places at number 3, with 8% of the votes.

2. 7 SECOND CHALLENGE WITH MIRANDA SINGS (ZOELLA)

When two queens of YouTube collab you get this kind of magic. With 12% of the votes, it's Zoella and Miranda Sings!

1. PHIL IS NOT ON FIRE (AMAZINGPHIL)

With 71% of the votes, the Phandom has spoken.

I'VE SEEN ___/50 OF THE BEST YOUTUBE VIDEOS OF ALL TIME!

THE HISTORY OF MIRANDA SINGS

Born just under a decade ago, Miranda Sings has been on a rollercoaster journey from talentless singer with a few followers to talentless singer with her very own Netflix show. Here's a look back at Miranda's best moments.

2008

FEB 2008: MIRANDA SINGS IS BORN
Comedian Coleen Ballinger creates her infamous alter-ego, to parody arrogant yet talentless singers who believed YouTube would bring them fame. It was a very different time.

MAR 2009: MIRANDA BLOWS UP!
Miranda's "Free Voice Lesson" video goes semi-viral; and she starts to make the character even more exaggerated.

2009

APR 2009: MIRANDA HITS THE ROAD
As Miranda starts touring the worldwide comedy circuit, BroadwayWorld.com calls her "the hottest, freshest and oddest breakout star in the scene".

2010: MIRANDA BECOMES A "FIVE-THREAT"
Miranda adds "magic" to her list of skills – which usually results in her stabbing herself in the neck with a sword.

2010

MAR 2010: MIRANDA AUDITIONS FOR GLEE
She was... unsuccessful.

MAY 2012: MIRANDA DOES NICKELODEON
Miranda "auditions" in a cameo in 'Victorious' – which stars real-life pal Ariana Grande.

2012

2013

MAR 2013: MIRANDA STARTS COLLABING
Her channel starts to blow up when she appears in videos with creators like Tyler Oakley and Bethany Mota.

APR 2014: MIRANDA HITS A MILLION
After years, Miranda hits her first million YouTube subscribers – and just keeps growing. For reference, she's currently close to 8 million.

2014

NOV 2014: MIRANDA VS. JERRY SEINFELD
Miranda confused the comedy legend and the rest of the world when she appeared as a guest on 'The Tonight Show Starring Jimmy Fallon'.

JUL 2015: MIRANDA WRITES A BOOK
Selp-Helf, a "decidedly unhelpful" lifestyle guide, is published and instantly becomes a NYT bestseller.

2015

2016

OCT 2016: MIRANDA GOES TO NETFLIX
'Haters Back Off' debuts as an original series that turns Miranda's dubious origins into a character-filled comedy.

2017: MIRANDA TAKES ON THE WORLD
With another tour, a second season of 'Haters Back Off' and her channel still growing, Miranda has become the unstoppable, if not questionably talented, superstar she always dreamed of being.

2017

12 TOTALLY TRUE "ALTERNATIVE FACTS" ABOUT YOUTUBERS

"Alternative facts" are everywhere. We can't live a single day without more things being exposed as "fake news" and would you believe it... YouTubers have been covering up this whole time, too. We've done some research and discovered 12 facts about 12 YouTubers they did NOT want you to know...

jacksepticeye's eyebrows are controlled by the government and transmit a complex series of codes about the location of nuclear warheads.

It's true

Patricia Bright's eyebrows are actually controlled by jacksepticeye.

Every hour, on the hour, Tyler Oakley must name one city from the United Arab Emirates. He's yet to explain why.

The Gabbie Show does not possess regular, functioning hips. It's how she's able to dance like that.

Louise Pentland turned Darcy into a Horcrux for reasons we'll never understand.

Liza Koshy lost the ability to care in an unfortunate boating accident back in 1962.

Todrick Hall can't sing a single note. He used the Sea Witch Ursula's powers to steal RuPaul's voice box and eventually came to be a megastar.

Dodie Clark is secretly made up of over 64% dork; making her illegal in most countries.

Jack Howard hates Dean Dobbs. Literally can't stand the guy.

Christine Sydelko has messed with Texas so many times that she's considered to be Public Enemy Number 1 over there.

Caspar Lee physically cannot function without Joe Sugg. He carries a small vial of Joe's blood around his neck at all times in case they stray too far away from each other.

Thomas Sanders was born when an overwhelming level of sadness was reached on Planet Earth. Thomas appeared to bring light back to our lives.

WHY ARE YOUTUBERS BEING CALLED "INFLUENCERS"?

"INFLUENCER" IS THE HOT NEW CATCH-ALL BUZZWORD FOR YOUTUBERS AND THEIR ILK. BUT IF YOU REALLY WANT THEM TO WORK WELL WITH YOU, THEN STOP CALLING THEM THAT.

If you've been orbiting around the YouTube sphere for as long as we have, you'll notice that every once in a while we enter a new era; another era, that is, of brands and digital businesses deliberately failing to understand the content creator game as they try their hardest to capitalise on it. The latest phase seems to have taken shape in a bizarre theory that online creators – people who make popular YouTube videos, or post stunning lifestyle Instagram photos, or do anything remotely creative in the social media sphere – don't actually take any pride in their work. That the goal, and ultimately the payoff, is having as large an audience as possible to do your bidding. That it's all about the influence.

As such, the exciting new catchall term "influencer" has gained traction amongst the more business-minded folks of the online world. The deeper you are involved with the YouTube industry, the more often you will likely hear this term; but the deeper you are involved with the YouTube community, the more it will likely give you the creeps.

A lot of you might be thinking "It's just a word, put your thought piece away," but as is always the response to that pithy argument: words have meaning, and power. The power that this particular umbrella term holds is the ability to compartmentalise and classify creators by what brands believe is their most marketable asset: their follower numbers. Their reach. Their demographic. Influence.

After this year's VidCon, I noticed "influencer" being used far more frequently than ever before; but a glaring discrepancy lay in who used the term. It rolled off the tongues of the employees of ad agencies, networks and digital brands; but anyone to whom the name "influencer" would apply seemed to steer well clear of it in conversations.

Of course, there are always going to be anomalies – a few years ago I saw a friend referring to themselves as a "social media influencer" on their LinkedIn. I assumed it was a joke (at the time my role was "Internet guy"), but evidently the phrase has since gained traction. We also recently saw comedian, actress and YouTuber Anna Akana refer to herself as an "influencer" in a lengthy rebuttal to Emma Thompson – but the important thing to note is this was part of a larger conversation about the value of online creators in the greater media sphere. Something that a phrase that leans heavily on the influence of a person fails to take into account.

Ultimately, my biggest beef with the phrase "influencer" is that it puts people who value their work, their identity, and yes, even their audience in the same box as faceless Twitter curators like @Dory and 'Common White Girl' – the owners of which earn five-figure sums by reposting relatable jokes they found on Tumblr.

If someone is willing to write a song, or direct a sketch, or even just talk to a camera about how much they think your product is the bee's knees, do they not deserve more than to be classed by how many pairs of eyes are going to be on it?

There is a nasty yet growing murmur of cynicism when it comes to the industry surrounding YouTubers and their like – brands believe they threw too much money at creators at the start, and now resent that they won't bend to their will with scripted phrases, impossible reshoots and week-long Twitter campaigns. But I believe there are still some of us out here with the crazy notion that what we make matters more to people than who we are. That even when working with a brand, our audiences can still trust us to create a genuine, relatable or evocative piece of digital content; and not just use our wealth in followers to push something we don't believe in for the cheque. And that is true influence.

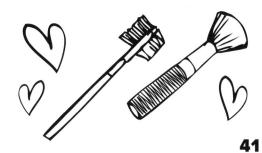

QUIZ: WHICH OF THESE YOUTUBERS HAVE NOT COLLABED?

CAN YOU GUESS WHICH CREATORS HAVEN'T MADE A VIDEO TOGETHER?

Collabs are a staple of the YouTube community; and at this point, it feels like every single YouTuber has collabed with each other at some point. But the truth is there are a handful who haven't yet crossed paths; so why not get them all together in a new quiz?

Time for you to test your knowledge of every YouTube collab under the sun. Can you come out of the other side with at least 8/10? Take the quiz and find out!

1 Who has Tyler Oakley missed guesting on his channel?

A Jon Cozart   **B** Tanya Burr   **C** Kingsley

2 Who hasn't had their PewDiePie collab debut?

A KSI   **B** Cryaotic   **C** CutiePieMarzia

3 Who's missing out of some Drunk Advice with Hannah Witton?

A Scola Dondo   **B** Lucy Moon   **C** Tim H

4 Who's hasn't popped up in an Anna Akana Sketch yet?

A Brizzy Voices   **B** Strawburry 17   **C** Mikey Murphy

Turn to page 93 for the answers!

5 Which of these ladies is missing out on some #GirlLove with Lilly Singh?

A Colleen Ballinger **B** Laci Green **C** Selena Gomez

6 Who isn't on Samantha Maria's collab list?

A Grace Victory **B** Fleur DeForce **C** Zoella

7 Who hasn't made sweet music with Dodie yet?

A Carrie Hope Fletcher **B** Meghan Tonjes **C** Jack Howard

8 Who hasn't had the pleasure of working with Thomas Sanders yet?

A Grace Helbig **B** Jon Cozart **C** BananaJamana

9 Who is missing the chance to goof on Eman Kellam's channel?

A Nathan Zed **B** TomSka **C** Ungespielt

10 Who's missing from Nathan Zed's channel?

A Savannah Brown **B** JacksFilms **C** JusReign

43

STOP READING NOW AND GO SUBSCRIBE TO THESE LIFESTYLE CHANNELS

There is a lot in this book about your YouTube faves – but there's always room in your subscription box to add some new faces. Here are just a handful of quick recommendations to get you started; and if you love lifestyle videos, we promise you won't be disappointed.

LIZA KOSHY

OK, she's a pretty big deal with millions of subscribers already but we predict HUGE things for Liza. Her humour, smile and talent shine through in every one of her videos and we're excited to see what she does next.

MSROSIEBEA

We've been following Rosie for several years, having spotted her on pixiwoo's Beauty Bootcamp in 2014. Lately we've been obsessed with Rosie's vlogs as she takes us along with her as she studies for a degree in Fashion Design.

HEY IT'S EMILY

First off, let's talk about that beautiful Irish accent – we melt. Secondly, Emily is just a great quality beauty YouTuber who never leaves us without a smile on our face and a super-long makeup wishlist.

LUCY WOOD

Lucy has one of the best smiles on YouTube. Fact. From her brilliant weekly vlogs (featuring everyone from Just Jodes to Gabriella Lindley) to high street hauls that make us want to go shopping ASAP, Lucy's channel is on the rise and will only continue to grow and grow.

ROBYN EEDE

Robyn features a whole lot of food on her channel. Simplifying the concept of veganism with easy-to-follow budget recipes and interesting food hauls, Robyn has been one of our favourite discoveries of the past twelve months.

MIKHILA MCDAID

Mikhila has been a YouTuber and blogger since 2010. With 94,000 followers to date, Mikhila's channel is perfect for fans of the drugstore and high street. From top products under a fiver to "wear and compare" videos and some good old-fashioned "empties" videos, you'll easily fall into a spiral of watching this channel for hours.

It's not like YouTubers ever um, what's the best way to describe it... 'massively exaggerate?' 'clickbait?' 'outright lie?' in their YouTube video titles. No, never. When you see the title "A stranger tried to grab me" it's not usually just a friend that tapped them to say hi on the street. When you see the title "I almost died", the video is never about tripping over, grazing your knee and getting straight back up. When you see the title "A barista attacked me", it's never just a story about a totally pleasant Starbucks worker saying hello. Eh, you've just got to take it all with a pinch of salt... right?

@httpzouwee   **Follow**

Cashier: your total is $45.82
Cashier: oops forgot to apply the discount, your total now is $38.53
Youtuber:

Story Time: I ALMOST GOT SCAMMED!

@httpzouwee/Twitter

jenny
@atwoodawson   **Follow**

hotel maid makes bed
youtuber:

CRAZY FAN BROKE INTO MY HOTEL: STORYTIME

@atwoodawson/Twitter

 adam
@polaxrize   **Follow**

youtuber: you brought me diet coke instead of regular coke
waiter: oh i'm sorry about that
youtuber:

I WAS POISONED | STORYTIME

@polaxrize/Twitter

 Chase Butler
@ChaseButlerTV   **Follow**

Kid: "Do you have any games on your phone?"
YouTuber:

SCARY Babysitting Story Time | "I Want To Play A Game..."

@ChaseButlerTV/Twitter

Tweet us @wetheunicorns with your funniest Story Time memes.

WHERE ARE ALL THE PLUS SIZE BRITISH YOUTUBERS?

A call out to all aspiring plus size vloggers!

Being a plus-size British woman who also runs a YouTube channel is actually pretty rare. Considering Internet stars like Callie Thorpe and George from Fuller Figure Fuller Bust have hit the mainstream, we're yet to see this really emulated on YouTube.

Diversity in the vlogging community is something we're passionate about. We really wanted to be able to showcase the top 10 British plus-size vloggers out there but, in truth, we were stumped. Where do Brit girls go online when they want to watch a Scarlett and Jo or ASOS Curve haul?

US viewers are spoilt for choice both with plus-size clothing stores and YouTubers. Sarah Rae Vargas, VintageOrTacky and LearningToBeFearless are great, to name a few. But wouldn't it be nice to see Brits whip out their lighting and vlog their own sassy style?

The British space isn't entirely empty and there are some brilliant British plus-size vloggers doing awesome things. Here are three favourites.

GRACE F VICTORY

A well-known name in the vlogging community is Grace F Victory. Packed with sass and confidence, Gracie's channel is empowering to say the least. With over 220,000 subscribers, Gracie is making an incredible impact in terms of diversity in the vlogging community.

SPRINKLEOFGLITTER

With 2.5 million subscribers, Louise is easily the most successful British plus-size YouTuber and her channel often features plus-size hauls and lookbooks, as well as regular chats about body image.

IT'S EM

Part of the StyleHaul gang, Emma's channel is the perfect mix of vlogs and plus-size style inspiration. Often teaming up with fellow YouTuber MsBudgetBeauty, their Style At Any Size series is a must-watch.

So this is a callout for all British plus-size YouTubers to make yourselves known and for plus-size females to let us know what they'd want to see more of online. Because if Unicorns can't change the world, who can? Tweet us @wetheunicorns.

IF FANDOMS' BRAINS WERE BROKEN DOWN INTO PIE CHARTS, THEY WOULD PROBABLY LOOK LIKE THIS...

These charts perfectly summarise *exactly* what thoughts take up what percentage of your brain on any given day.

What percentage of a YouTube fan's brain thinks about which topics? We've worked it all out and put the info in to some helpful pie charts for you.

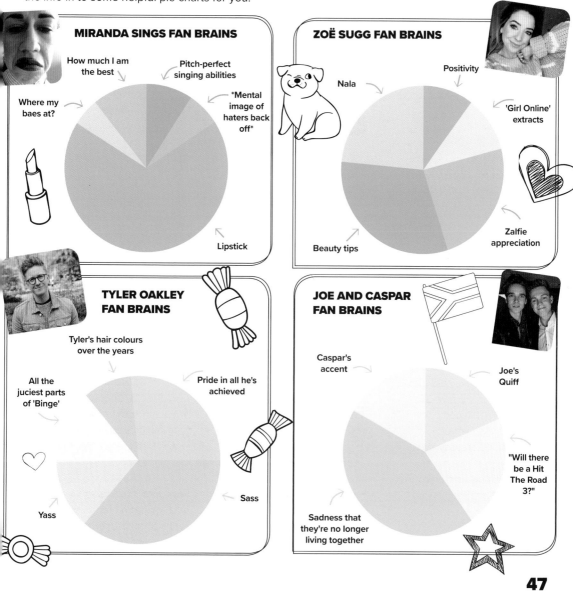

MIRANDA SINGS FAN BRAINS

- How much I am the best
- Pitch-perfect singing abilities
- *Mental image of haters back off*
- Where my baes at?
- Lipstick

ZOË SUGG FAN BRAINS

- Positivity
- Nala
- 'Girl Online' extracts
- Zalfie appreciation
- Beauty tips

TYLER OAKLEY FAN BRAINS

- Tyler's hair colours over the years
- Pride in all he's achieved
- All the juiciest parts of 'Binge'
- Sass
- Yass

JOE AND CASPAR FAN BRAINS

- Caspar's accent
- Joe's Quiff
- "Will there be a Hit The Road 3?"
- Sadness that they're no longer living together

SEVEN THINGS YOUR PARENTS HAVE DEFINITELY SAID ABOUT YOUTUBE

'YOU'RE A FAN OF THAT DAN AND BILL AREN'T YOU?'

You're a fun youth; you enjoy music, friends and YouTubers. You're hip, you're cool, you have a razor scooter and a bucket hat, you're down with the sickness. You just get it – but hey, you know who doesn't get it? That's right – ya parents. We can almost guarantee these words have passed through your parents sweet lips at some point or another.

1. "WHAT IS VLOGGING?"

If you ask your parents to describe what they think a vlogger is, they can probably give you all the ingredients: it involves cameras, people film 'in their room', they 'don't really do anything' (their words not ours). Despite all this, though, they still do not truly comprehend what it's all about.

2. "AND THEY ACTUALLY MAKE MONEY DOING THIS?"

Yes Mum. Yes, that much. Adverts on the videos, Mum. Yes I have considered getting into it myself.

3. "YOU'RE A FAN OF DAN AND BILL, AREN'T YOU?"

It's Dan and Phil. You know this, we know this, and the Dalai Llama knows this – but your parents? Nope. It's hard to know why your parents are incapable of learning two very common names, and yet the ability entirely escapes them. It might as well be Chinese as far as your dad is concerned.

4. "DID YOU KNOW THAT THAT ZOOELLA HAS HER OWN PRODUCTS?!"

"I saw them in Boots! She must be making a fortune!"

5. "WHY DON'T YOU WATCH SOME REAL TV?"

It's strange that television, once the scourge of parents, has now become the respectable media source compared to the crazy world of YouTube. If this keeps up, it won't be long before you're yelling at your own kids: "get off that holodeck and come and watch some PINOF like a grown-up!".

6. "I THINK IT'S A NICE THING FOR YOU TO BE INTO."

This one is a little cheesy, but we hope it applies to you. In our experience, we've found that parents seem to be overjoyed that their kids are involved in a community that's friendly, creative and open-minded.

7. 'POOTYPIE, BOOBYGUY, CUTIEPIE ETC, ETC.'

Look, we know that PewDiePie isn't the most conventional name in the world, so we can kind of forgive the parents for not being able to quite nail this one. To be honest 'that loud Swedish guy' is close enough, so we think we'll give them a pass this time.

BINGO! YOUTUBE ANNOUNCEMENT EDITION

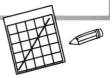

Sick of "BIG announcements"? Play the game with us!

If you enjoyed playing Bingo: The YouTube Drama Edition on page 28, it's time for another round. You already know how it works — but with this one there's a twist — it's to be played whenever a YouTuber declares they have a "BIG ANNOUNCEMENT". Is it a book? A tour? An engagement? Who cares, you'll have more fun playing the game.

How to play: *the boring bit zzzzz*

- Check off a box whenever you see/hear the relevant thing happen.
- Continue as necessary until you check off five boxes in a row: horizontal, vertical and diagonal all apply.
- The FREE SPACE allows you to complete a row that passes through the middle for free.
- HARD MODE: Go for a Full House (checking off every box).

IT'S A BOOK	ANNOUNCEMENT HAPPENS JUST IN TIME FOR CHRISTMAS (CONVENIENT!)	THERE'S A KICKSTARTER INVOLVED SOMEHOW	ACTUALLY WASN'T THAT BIG AN ANNOUNCEMENT REALLY	"DOING THIS HAS BEEN MY DREAM FOR SO LONG!"
"I ACTUALLY WROTE/ DESIGNED THIS MYSELF!"	THEY'RE SELLING MORE MERCH	KEEPS TWEETING ABOUT THE BIG ANNOUNCEMENT	"I'VE HAD TO KEEP THIS A SECRET FOR AGES!"	EVENT/POSTAGE ISN'T HAPPENING ANYWHERE NEAR WHERE YOU LIVE
"I'M WORKING WITH A GREAT TEAM OF PEOPLE TO MAKE THIS HAPPEN"	JOKES ABOUT HAVING A BOOK, PROMOTES SOMETHING ELSE	**FREE SPACE!**	THE ANNOUNCEMENT VIDEO ENDS UP BEING A BIT LATE	MISLEADING THUMBNAIL OR TITLE
EVERYBODY HAD FIGURED IT OUT ALREADY	"ARE YOU ALL EXCITED FOR MY BIG ANNOUNCEMENT LATER?!"	IT'S NOT A BOOK/ TOUR/MERCH ANNOUNCEMENT	IT'S A SECOND CHANNEL	"I COULDN'T HAVE DONE THIS WITHOUT YOU GUYS!"
FANS ACT SUPER ANNOYED	FANS ACT, LIKE, FRIGHTENINGLY EXCITED ABOUT IT	THE BIG ANNOUNCEMENT COUNTDOWN ALONE LASTS OVER A WEEK	CRYING HAPPENS	THEY'RE GOING ON A TOUR

YOUTUBERS ADMIT TO FORCING HAPPINESS; BUT WHAT DOES THAT MEAN?

IT'S TIME TO TALK ABOUT POSITIVITY.

Whether it's in real life or in the videos we watch, it's not unusual to hear people describe YouTubers as having the perfect life. Thanks to vlogging talents and the skills to edit an entire day's worth of footage down to 5-10 minutes, an over-arching feeling of happiness seems to radiate out of YouTube. But despite appearances, we never truly take the time to wonder: are these people just as positive and peppy once the camera is switched off? To explore this question we've taken a look at four of the most popular videos on the topic as the likes of PewDiePie, Casey Neistat, Shane Dawson and Scola Dondo weighed in on the issue of mental health.

PEWDIEPIE – 'FORCED POSITIVITY ON YOUTUBE'

In this video, Felix talks about how he used to over-hype his reactions to games, but that as soon as he stopped recording, he'd be in a bad mood. Because of this change fans have come to believe that Felix is unhappy simply because he has stopped forcing a peppy attitude on camera. On the topic of other creators who "act happy", he believes they are "forcing positivity to get more views on YouTube".

In addition to talking about his own change of perspective, he bashes motivational posters and speakers for saying that the best way to improve your life is to convince yourself to be happy. He states that filtering one's life and broadcasting only the highlights to an audience of potentially millions is "dishonest" and is doing "more harm than good".

CASEY NEISTAT – 'I'M NOT THAT HAPPY'

Next up is Casey Neistat who discusses how, over 600 days, he filmed and worked 20-hour days to "pluck the happy and fun and interesting aspects of [my] life" and put it onto YouTube. He discusses how during this time, he obviously had "fights with [his] wife" and attended a funeral that he had to consciously vlog around because his audience didn't need to see the negative parts of his life.

Most importantly of all, Casey mentions how, now that he's not vlogging daily, he has a lot more "free brain space" to "return to being a human being". If the King of Daily Vlogging tells you that being a YouTuber made him feel inhuman, then you need to hear what else he's saying: shrinking his life down into 10 minute videos of concentrated happiness made him feel genuinely awful.

SHANE DAWSON – 'WHY YOUTUBERS ARE DEPRESSED'

Shane's video is longer than other YouTubers' vlogs talking about the topic of forced positivity, but focuses on a different angle entirely. He uploaded it after fans asked why he didn't appear in YouTube Rewind 2016, and explains how "most YouTubers aren't even themselves in their videos that much". Shane makes specific reference to the concept of meeting YouTubers in real life, and how most people realise how human and "sad" they come across in comparison to their video personas – BECAUSE of the way they force an image of happiness.

On a personal level, he discusses the difficulty that comes with creating videos and then having to "edit" and stare at yourself for hours on end every single day. This is a struggle for Shane, who has been open about his body image issues in the past, and it has been the main reason he has turned down opportunities such as YouTube Rewind. It's reasons like this that Shane believes "YouTubers are depressed".

SCOLA DONDO – 'WHY I'M NOT HAPPY'

And finally, Scola Dondo uploaded her "confession" regarding her own emotions as a YouTuber. In her words, "everyone on YouTube seems to have some sort of mental health problem" and at the beginning of her own career, "it took a little while to figure out" her own depression. In fact, Scola admits to faking "being positive and [...] happy" in the past to conceal her true emotions.

Scola goes on to explain why she does this and why "particular personality traits" seem more popular on YouTube. She's been told in the past by fans that she's "a lot shyer in person" based on the way she films herself "in [her] most comfortable state". She says that: "Odds are, I'm turning on the camera when I'm in my best mood, and so you're seeing the happiest version of myself".

QUIZ: CAN YOU GUESS THESE YOUTUBERS FROM OUR TERRIBLE DRAWINGS?

WE HAVE SERIOUSLY GOOD DRAWING SKILLS.

We can do many things: we can write books and articles, we can report YouTuber news, we cna do gud speling – but drawing? Not so much. Here at Unicorns HQ we've got out our pencils and created a batch of ~~truly terrible~~ absolutely amazing YouTuber art. Can you guess who is who? When you're done join in the fun and tweet us your own horrible artistic creation.

1

A   Tanya Burr
B   Fleur DeForce
C   Zoë Sugg

2

A   Dan Howell
B   Connor Franta
C   Phil Lester

3

A   Ricky Dillon
B   Joey Graceffa
C   Tyler Oakley

4

A   Nathan Zed
B   Michael from Vsauce
C   Jonathan Saccone Joly

Turn to page 93 for the answers!

5

A   Liam Dryden
B   Dodie Clark
C   Ingrid Nilsen

6

A   Both of the Fine Bros
B   Miranda Sings
C   Carrie Hope Fletcher

7

A   Chris Kendall
B   KickThePj
C   Phil Lester

DRAW YOUR FAVE HERE AND SHARE YOUR CREATION WITH US USING THE HASHTAG #BADYOUTUBERART

THERE ARE
SEVEN KINDS OF YOUTUBE FANS...

WHICH ONE ARE YOU?

1 THE HATE WATCHER

You don't subscribe to YouTubers, and you don't even LIKE YouTubers, but you can't stop watching them. You're fascinated by just watching how they talk and act, even though it ticks you off to the high heavens — but oh well, you love spilling the tea with your mates about that awful YouTuber's latest video. Unfortunately, this is one of the most difficult and testing kinds of YouTube fan, because before you realise it... you might just turn into their biggest fan!

2 THE DIEHARD FAN

Let's be real, as much as you tell all your friends and family that you're the biggest YouTube fan in the world, you only watch one person and they're your entire life. You've seen every video, collab, Snapchat, background and indirect they've ever been in and you're more than happy to spend your days memorising absolutely everything about their lives. In fact, you probably know more about their life than the creator does themselves.

3 THE HOPELESSLY ROMANTIC

For you it's very difficult to find the line between avid viewer and actually in a relationship with something. There's a 90% chance you're mentally in a committed partnership with someone you subscribe to, even if they're not totally aware of it yet. Your walls are covered in posters. Your social media platforms are just glorified fan accounts. But finally, and more painfully, you've cried more than once when you've met them IRL.

me + phil

4 THE NOTIFICATION CREW

You're more professional than The Diehard and Hopelessly Romantic kinds of fans, because you're legit. You belong to The Notification Crew and are fully committed to watching your favourite YouTubers the very SECOND they upload their latest video. Being part of the NC isn't easy, and may require sneaky breaks to the bathroom during classes and presentations to make sure you're the first on Twitter to tweet out those brand new in-jokes, but it's a lifestyle you're totally committed to.

5 THE FIGHTER

You've been a part of most of these types of YouTube fandoms; you've been there for the notifications, you've been madly in love with a creator before and there was a stage in your life when you owned the most popular YouTuber fan account in the world... but now things have changed. Now you're just angry and ready to fight anyone willing to attack your fave, regardless of who gets caught up in the drama. You're here to see how you can spread the salt and are known as the ONE fan in your community that should not be crossed.

6 THE TIRED BLOGGER

This is by far one of the most testing kinds of fans, because you're the one who stays up late into the night GIF-ing everyone's favourite videos and creating memes out of tweets. You're famous on Tumblr and iconic on Twitter, but it's a thankless job. Because of you, in-jokes and memes stay a loveable part of any fandom, but it comes at a cost – you've not seen daylight for weeks and your Giphy account is reaching its capacity. We salute you.

7 THE CURIOUS VIEWER

You're perhaps new to the world of YouTube. You kinda like the way vlogs are made, and you definitely want to be a YouTuber yourself one day, but you're still not entirely sure if it's your cup of tea. It's new and unusual, but it's a fascinating world you want to learn more about. Instead of subscribing to creators, leaving comments or getting involved in the community, you prefer to sleuth around the edges, watching videos in your free time and silently judging everybody.

QUIZ: CAN YOU SPOT WHICH YOUTUBER IS THE ODD ONE OUT?

We all think we know YouTubers, but can you spot the odd one out? Do you know who has been in a major film, who has pets or who has appeared in a music video?

1 Which one is the odd one out?

A
Miranda Sings

B
Cameron Dallas

C
Anna Saccone

2 Which one is the odd one out?

A
Safiya Nygaard

B
Sophie Foster

C
Liza Koshy

3 Which one is the odd one out?

A
Victoria Magrath

B
David Dobrik

C
Samantha Maria

4 Which one is the odd one out?

A
Mark Ferris

B
Patricia Bright

C
Shirley B. Eniang

Turn to page 93 for the answers!

5 Which one is the odd one out?

A
Joey Graceffa

B
Roman Atwood

C
Jesse Wellens

6 Which one is the odd one out?

A
Anna Akana

B
Troye Sivan

C
Emma Blackery

7 Which one is the odd one out?

A
Markiplier

B
Manny Mua

C
Michelle Phan

8 Which one is the odd one out?

A
Sean Elliott OC

B
Gabriella
Lindley

C
Tanya Burr

YOU CAN DISAGREE WITH A YOUTUBER AND STILL BE A FAN

Fans of creators have been fighting over criticism of their faves – but here's why nobody is in the wrong.

In early 2017 there was a lot of debate surrounding PewDiePie and a controversial video he made which divided his fan base. There were numerous fans commenting that they were "disappointed" that Felix had made this video. In response, other fans would jump in and say that they can't be a fan if they didn't like that video. It was an assertion that you're only a true fan of someone if you never disagree with them. But the thing is – that's just not true.

YOU CAN DISLIKE AN ACTION AND STILL LIKE THE PERSON

YouTubers are people; they are imperfect and make mistakes just like the rest of us. So while that doesn't mean that their mistakes should be instantly forgiven, it also doesn't necessarily mean they should never be forgiven. In an ideal world, if a creator makes a mistake, they will be self-aware enough to admit it and rectify it. For example: Markiplier, someone who is very clearly not a homophobe, was recently accused of being homophobic; but he demonstrated through his later actions, in raising thousands for a LGBTQ+ charity, that this was clearly not the case. After this, he and his fandom were able to happily move forward. It becomes more grey when a YouTuber makes a misstep (or what you personally perceive as a misstep) and is unapologetic. It then becomes a matter of your personal conscience and choice, as to whether you support them. PewDiePie has insisted that he wasn't trying to promote a hate message; but has not apologised for displaying the message. It is then up to you to decide whether you remain a fan and disagree with that action, or agree with him, or just stop being a fan. But the point is, none are necessarily the correct option. You have to weigh it up and decide for yourself.

ARE THERE EXCEPTIONS? OF COURSE THERE ARE

There are, as with anything in life, exceptions to this rule. There are some actions that creators can take that mean that it becomes impossible for certain people to be able to support them any more. For example, we found that many of you responded to JonTron's controversial opposition of The Women's March, by saying that you could never watch him again. Even more extreme, when a YouTuber does something truly shocking, it is expected that even the most hardcore of their fandom will turn away from them.

What we are ultimately trying to say here is that YouTubers, like any public figure, should be held up to your own personal standards; and if you feel that they have crossed a line, you don't 'owe' it to them to overlook it or be okay with it, if it is not okay for you. By the same token, if you can disagree with a certain action but make your peace with still being a fan, then go for it; and don't let anyone accuse you of not being a 'real' fan.

CAN YOU TAKE ON THE
#TENCHANNELCHALLENGE?

Who are your top ten YouTubers with under 100k subscribers?

Here at Unicorns we want to give you guys all the news about the YouTubers you love, but we also believe one of the most important parts of the online community is that everyone is given a voice, no matter how big their audience is. In that spirit, we have devised a brand new challenge. We're calling it – the **#TenChannelChallenge**. To take part in the challenge all you have to do is subscribe to ten YouTubers who have less than 100,000 subscribers. Here are some of our favourites.

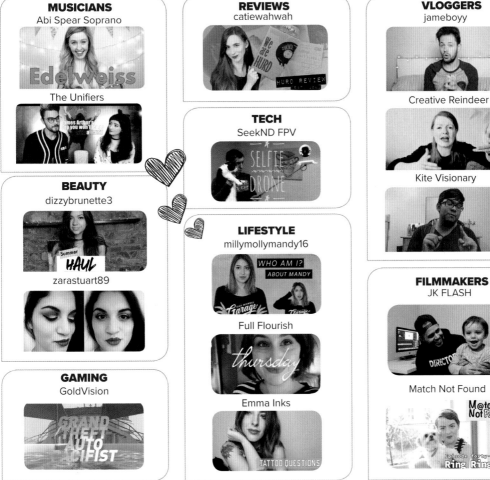

MUSICIANS
Abi Spear Soprano

The Unifiers

BEAUTY
dizzybrunette3

zarastuart89

GAMING
GoldVision

REVIEWS
catiewahwah

TECH
SeekND FPV

LIFESTYLE
millymollymandy16

Full Flourish

Emma Inks

VLOGGERS
jameboyy

Creative Reindeer

Kite Visionary

FILMMAKERS
JK FLASH

Match Not Found

Make sure to share your #TenChannelChallenge selection with us @wetheunicorns!

QUIZ: IS THIS A SCREENSHOT FROM A DAN VIDEO, OR A PHIL VIDEO?

TIME TO TEST YOUR DEEP, DEEP PHANDOM.

Can you tell which channel a video has come from just by looking at a single frame on it? Most people could not – but the Phandom? We have a funny feeling they might just be able to.

1

☐ Dan video   ☐ Phil video

2

☐ Dan video   ☐ Phil video

3

☐ Dan video   ☐ Phil video

4

☐ Dan video   ☐ Phil video

Turn to page 93 for the answers!

5

☐ Dan video   ☐ Phil video

6

☐ Dan video   ☐ Phil video

7

☐ Dan video   ☐ Phil video

REAL TALK: SUBSCRIBER COUNT MEANS NOTHING THESE DAYS

You've been able to subscribe to people on YouTube pretty much since day one. Creators are often applauded and placed in levels of fame based on their subscriber count. And, for upcoming creators, setting and smashing subscriber milestones is one of the most rewarding things in the world... but if you stop and think about it, subscriber counts are pretty useless.

First off, let's point out that there was no distinct moment in time when the "subscribe" function stopped being so powerful. To this day, people still stare in awe at the likes of Smosh and PewDiePie for their unbelievable subscriber count. The problem is however, that these channels often get only a fraction of the views they should be getting if every single one of their subscribers actually clicked on each video they uploaded.

To be honest, there's now such a discrepancy between the amount of subscribers and the amount of views any channel receives that it's almost laughable. Even PewDiePie, the guy on YouTube with the highest subscriber count at over 55 million subscribers, touched upon how

useless this number was in a video all about deleting his YouTube channel.

Unfortunately for Felix, 55 million subscribers does not mean 55 million views on his videos. As with your cable membership, you'll be paying a fee for hundreds of channels at a time, but are you going to watch them all?

No, but you pay regardless to have access to them. This thought process applies to YouTube creators as well, who may have people subscribe to their channel but not necessarily view every single upload.

This lack of engagement can be seen when YouTubers do brand deals. Marketing companies often sign creators up based on their subscriber count and "potential reach", but underestimate the amount of people that will actually watch a video, let alone one that's clearly marked as an ad. More creators nowadays are basing the health of their channel on how many views their recent videos get (and not old viral successes), because their subscriber numbers have come to mean diddly-squat.

If you look at Tyler Oakley: with 7.9 million subscribers, he's arguably one of the most famous YouTubers alive, and yet his recent uploads haven't hit the millions of views you might expect.

YouTube users have been plagued for years by various faults with algorithms, subscriber glitches and a lack of videos in their subscription feeds, but this only echoes the idea that the need to subscribe to channels in 2017 is pointless. With the introduction of the bell feature, so fans can be notified when new videos are uploaded, surely YouTube has technically admitted themselves that subscribing means nothing nowadays?

On the other hand, smaller channels may see a strong correlation between their subscriber count and their video views because such a focused audience will inevitably be more dedicated. But channels such as PewDiePie that undeniably have dead/fake accounts inflating their subscribers will never be able to match their data. Unfortunately, "only 1% of viewers tend to interact with a video".

Alexys (Lex) Fleming ✔
@MadeULookbyLex
➕ Follow

"We are living in a world of view count, subscriber count, and not in a world of creation or awesome content anymore."
@MadeULookbyLex/Twitter

Alexys (MadeYewLook) Fleming made it clear that regardless of your view count or subscriber count, creators should just continue making the videos they love and the rest should fall into place. Instead of fussing over their subscriber count, they should focus on their views instead. Better views means a more engaged fan base, a much wider sphere of influence and a higher chance to increase your revenue. The amount of people subscribed to your channel will not do any of these things and will only serve to make you compare yourself to other channels. Concentrate on your output and creativity, and maybe stop breaking your back over trying to get yourself one of these shiny YouTube Play Buttons.

WHAT IS SELF CARE AND HOW DO YOU DO IT?

HERE'S SOME VITAL INFORMATION AND INSPIRATION.

'Self care' is a term you might have seen being used in YouTube videos, on social media and in articles. Self care has quickly become the thing we're all trying to achieve and make space for on our ever-growing to do lists. So what is it? Well, self care basically means taking time for yourself and your own mental health. It sounds so easy, right? But when you're drowning in studies and/or work, seeing friends, family duties and not to mention the mundane stuff in life like cleaning and life admin then looking after ourselves becomes last on the list. Self care is about more than making sure your hair looks neat and getting an early night once in a blue moon, it's about keeping your mental health in check – no matter whether you suffer from mental health problems or not.

HERE ARE A FEW EXAMPLES OF WHAT YOUR YOUTUBE FAVES DO WHEN THEY NEED SOME SELF CARE TIME:

Tyler Oakley ✓
@tyleroakley   👤 Follow ∨

"today i'm gonna focus on self-care & do things that make me smile – not to distract me from our reality, but to sprinkle my own magic on top"
@tyleroakley/Twitter

Let's Talk About Self Care

Louise Pentland and Catrific do an amazing job of explaining the concept in their video: 'Let's Talk About Self Care'.

Rosianna Halse Rojas ✓
@papertimelady   👤 Follow ∨

"Started running again this morning. So begin[s] 31 days of intense self care and good habit developing!"
@papertimelady/Twitter

Callie ✓
@CallieThorpe   👤 Follow ∨

"Gunna do some self care stuff tonight because stress levels are 100 again. Face mask, wine, SATC box set.

Q is What takeaway shall I have?"
@CallieThorpe/Twitter

Jake Edwards
@jakeftmagic   👤 Follow ∨

"*slips into bed at 10.30pm with a caffeinated beverage* SELF CARE"
@jakeftmagic/Twitter

  Gracie 🖤 ✓
@GraceFVictory
👤 Follow ⌄

"Today's self care; galaxy chocolate and a cuppa tea, a new Netflix series, a calming room spray & burning sage"
@GraceFVictory/Twitter

 Rosianna Halse Rojas ✓
@papertimelady

"Self care."
@papertimelady/Twitter

Looking for more info? Everyone from Grace Victory to Tyler Oakley and Laci Green have made some awesome videos that will inspire you and help you think about what you need to do to make sure you're the very best version of you. Check out their videos.

Lex Croucher ✓
@lexcanroar
👤 Follow ⌄

"a little bit of self care goes a long way. had my nails done + mindfulness meditation + a bath last night and I feel so light today"
@lexcanroar/Twitter

Beckie Jane Brown ✓
@BeckieJBrown
👤 Follow ⌄

"No one from the crew wants to go to Disney (or with me if they are) – so I'm headed alone. Thank goodness I'm strong enough to do it!"
@BeckieJBrown/Twitter

Rowan Ellis ✓
@HeyRowanEllis
👤 Follow ⌄

"@BeckieJBrown doing Disney alone was good self care for me last year, plus you can use single rider lines and only have to queue for 5 mins!"
@HeyRowanEllis/Twitter

'HOW TO SELF CARE?!'
– lacigreen

'Looking After Yourself, Self Care & Happiness'
– Grace F Victory

'5 Easy Self-Care Tips'
– Tyler Oakley

65

THE 10 BEST BOOKTUBERS TO WATCH WHEN HIBERNATING

Get a blanket and settle down for this read!

These BookTubers will make you feel less guilty about staying in all day with your feet up. So if you've got the kettle boiling and you're nice and comfy, it's worth checking them out.

1. SUNBEAMSJESS

Jess vlogs book hauls that she has bought, been given, or been sent by publishers. She's been a bookworm vlogger since she was 16 but recieved a huge following after Tanya Burr promoted her on her channel, because of her beauty vlogs. She also has an everyday vlogging channel called extrasunbeamsjess.

2. JEN CAMPBELL

London living vlogger Jen talks about novels, short stories and poems on her channel, as well as doing collaborations with other BookTubers throughout the month. Jen has also written her own bestselling novel on the 'Weird Things Customers Say in Bookshops'.

3. GOWITHFLICK

GoWithFlick, (Felicity Grace) started her YouTube channel four years ago creating her vlogging channel MoreFlick, where she vlogs about her days out with friends and family and her many shopping trips.

4. BENJAMINOFTOMES

This blogger, vlogger and publisher, is also known for his Instagram. With artsy bookstagram photos he's wracked up over 65,000 followers who just can't get enough of his cheerful self. His videos are bound to make you feel good.

5. BOOKS BEAUTY AMERIIE

As BookTubers go, Ameriie is a diverse one. She is a huge bookworm but also loves to vlog about fashion, she sings and has frequent make-up tutorials. She does what she loves and clearly people are loving her content as she has over 36,000 subscribers.

6. ROSE READS

As with many BookTubers, Rose is a lover of writing, and is an author who got her own publishing deal at the young age of just 19. She now writes her blog, posts regularly on YouTube and writes her Young Adult fantasy trilogy, Roses.

7. CHARR FREARS

Charr is a graduate of English who loves to vlog about the books she's excited for, the shopping trips and hauls of novels she's picked up and everything on her TBR lists. She also is an advocate of body confidence and mental health awareness.

8. BOOKSANDQUILLS

Sanne Vliegenthart is behind Books and Quills. Originally from the Netherlands, Sanne moved to London a few years ago to get her dream job working for the hub of novels, Penguin Random House. Sanne is the perfect BookTuber to

watch when its cold and rainy outside, with candles on snuggled up in a blanket burrito.

9. KATIE RUBY

Katie is a creative writing graduate from Yorkshire who loves to vlog about comic books and her travels. Watching her videos is a sure-fire way of giving yourself wanderlust.

10. JEAN BOOKISHTHOUGHTS

London PhD student Jean vlogs about the best books to read during different times of year: from scary books at Halloween to Non-Fiction November.

PEWDIEPIE HAS MORE SUBSCRIBERS THAN THESE HUGE COUNTRIES HAVE PEOPLE

Canada? Seriously?!

PewDiePie has 55,230,827 YouTube subscribers (at the time of print), which means he has more subscribers than over 160 actual countries have people. Here's an infographic of some of the most surprising ones.

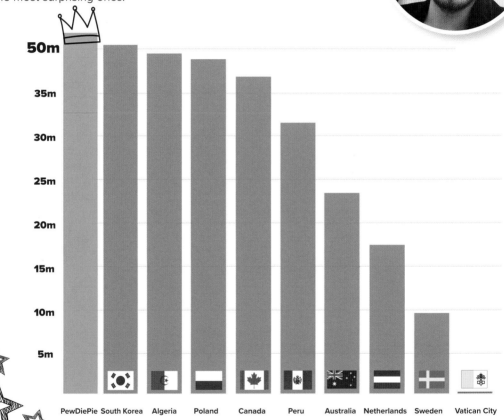

| | PewDiePie | South Korea | Algeria | Poland | Canada | Peru | Australia | Netherlands | Sweden | Vatican City |

Now, you may argue that although he has **55 million+ subscribers, that number may be inaccurate due to unused accounts, people with multiple accounts etc. etc. But consider this – even if half, HALF of PewDiePie's subscribers aren't real, you would only subtract the first 25 countries from the list of 160 – and his channel would still be THREE TIMES more populous than his home country of Sweden. Insane.**

QUIZ: CAN YOU MATCH THE YOUTUBER TO THE COUNTRY THEY WERE BORN IN?

If we had to give you one piece of advice when taking this quiz, it would be – think carefully how you choose your answer. Some of these may seem incredibly obvious – even too obvious – but that's what makes them so devious! Look at the list of YouTuber's below, and then write the correct name beneath the flag. Good luck!

Turn to page 93 for the answers!

1. Flula Borg
2. Lilly Singh
3. Marzia Bisognin

4. Felix Kjellberg
5. Anna Saccone
6. Caspar Lee

7. Troye Sivan
8. Liam Dryden
9. Darude

CANADA

SWEDEN
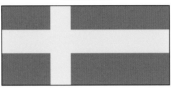

FINLAND

ENGLAND

ITALY

SOUTH AFRICA

SCOTLAND

GERMANY

USA

GLOW UP

Everyone loves a good #TBT, especially when those throw backs are completely awkward. Here's a throwback to what your favourite creators looked like years ago when MySpace was king and bad eyeliner was a thing.

THEN

ZOELLA

NOW

CASPAR LEE

THEN

NOW

JOE SUGG

THEN

NOW

SPRINKLEOFGLITTER

THEN

NOW

OLI WHITE

THEN

NOW

TOMSKA

THEN

NOW

HOW MUCH DOES BEING A YOUTUBER AFFECT YOUR MENTAL HEALTH?

ARE THE TWO CONNECTED?

YouTube creators are finally opening up by the dozens about their struggles with depression and anxiety; but why does Internet fame seem to attract mental illness so much? With many of our favourite creators sharing words of support on World Mental Health Day, it's reassuring to see just how far the YouTube community has come.

Zoë ✓
@Zoella

👤 Follow ∨

"To my lovely followers who suffer in some way on a daily basis. YOU ARE NOT YOUR MENTAL ILLNESS! Speak out! Support! #WorldMentalHealthDay"
@Zoella/Twitter

In October 2016 Zoella posted a meaty update on her site, talking in detail about her anxiety for the first time in a couple of years. She recounts growing up with it, and the ways in which she had to make drastic changes as she quickly became the sensation we all know today.

"Some weeks I'd feel on top of the world, and other weeks I would be rocking back and fourth in tears on a train on my own on my way to London to film something," she admits in the post. "Although I never really talked in depth about my anxiety and the rise of my channel at the time, it was something that was extremely challenging to balance." (zoella.co.uk)

After sticking to a rigorous therapy schedule and stepping well outside her comfort zone, Zoë's made a lot of progress in recent months; and she would recommend therapy to anyone.

"We look after our skin, our hair, we go to the gym, the dentist, we focus on eating the right foods but how often do we spend time looking after the one thing that requires us to fully function in the way we do?" (zoella.co.uk)

Zoë has admitted to dealing with forms of anxiety well before she made a name for herself online; but with more and more YouTubers opening up about their own struggles all the time, it does beg the question: how much does YouTube and mental illness go hand in hand?

Last year Charlie McDonnell opened up about dealing with anxiety and depression for almost as long as he has been creating videos on the site. He made the important distinction of "separating yourself from the illness"

(charlieissocoollike/YouTube) – and inspired a newly nuanced way of being open about mental health online.

The obvious connection to make is that the pressures of fame will have a major contributing factor in mental illness; indeed, there have been an infinite number of studies and examples of how fame can have a direct affect on mental health. But in the case of YouTube, with many examples of creators getting into YouTube already dealing with their own issues, one does have to wonder how this career seems to attract those who already have a lot on their plate.

Surprisingly, some insight to this comes from one particular quote from the Mental Health panel at Summer in the City 2016. During the discussion, panel contributor TomSka declared "I make the videos I wanted and needed to see when I was 14." While on its own this is a powerful image of Tom's relationship with himself, it also taps into the idea of connectivity.

While many creators don't necessarily feel okay all the time, it's important to them that others who feel the same know that they aren't alone. Many creators who have been around as long as Charlie, Tom or Zoë, joined YouTube not with the intent to become famous, but to connect with others over a shared passion. And with the rapid de-stigmatisation of discussing mental health, they have found a new role in becoming the voice of support they didn't have at an earlier age.

Are online fame and mental illness connected? Most likely. But that costly connection is also one of its greatest benefits; as where we previously had a silent few, we now have the tools to help millions.

THE COMPLETE TIMELINE OF
DIL HOWLTER

The short but epic life story of the Phandom's favourite Sim.

Dil Howlter has had a heck of a life since Dan and Phil spawned him from the best parts of themselves in 'The Sims 4'. Here is a look back at some of the digital dreamboat's highlights.

2014

SEPTEMBER 24TH 2014:
DIL HOWLTER IS BORN
A hero for the ages, a man for all seasons – Dil Howlter is born and is ready to take the world of The Sims by storm.

OCTOBER 25TH 2014:
DIL MAKES HIS FIRST ENEMY
Things get off to a rough start as Dil begins to battle Erica, who would go on to become a long-running archenemy.

NOVEMBER 8TH 2014:
DIL NEARLY DIES
Dil is electrocuted whilst trying to repair a radio.

DECEMBER 23RD 2014:
DILCAKES WAS BORN... AND THEN DIED
Eliza Pancakes, the love that never truly was. Dil is rejected at the park – but also, Eliza is freakin' married so it was kinda inevitable.

JANUARY – APRIL 2015:
FOUR HUNDRED BILLION HILARIOUS THINGS HAPPEN
Too many zany capers to record in one list.

2015

APRIL 14TH 2015:
DIL MEETS TABITHA
Little did we know how historic this meeting would be – the start of a whole new chapter in Dil's life. Welcome Tabitha Casper to the story.

JULY 10TH 2015:
TABITHA DISAPPEARS... AND THEN REAPPEARS
What a rollercoaster ride; after an ill-conceived camping excursion, Tabitha was nowhere to be found. Then she came back... somehow.

SEPTEMBER 24TH 2015:
DIL CELEBRATES HIS FIRST BIRTHDAY
Our little guy is all grown up. Time to re-watch his birthday video and celebrate Dil's big day all over again.

DECEMBER 21ST 2015:
DIL AND TABITHA SPEND THE NIGHT TOGHETHER
Netflix and Dil becomes a reality.

2016

SEPTEMBER 11TH 2016:
DIL GETS MARRIED
Dil and Tabitha finally tie the knot, and there wasn't a dry eye in the house.

DECEMBER 4TH 2016:
TABITHA BECOMES PREGNANT
All that Netflix and Dil'ing paid off!.

DECEMBER 14TH 2016:
DIL AND TABITHA BECOME PARENTS
Little baby Dab Howlter! Congrats, Dil!

HOW TO SUCCEED AS A SMALLER YOUTUBER

"THERE'S A MISCONCEPTION THAT A SMALL YOUTUBER IS A NEW YOUTUBER OR AN UNSUCCESSFUL YOUTUBER. SOME OF US ARE JUST HAPPY BEING SMALLER."

Summer in the City hosts panels of all kinds from comedy to music to calling people out online. The common theme on all of these panels, however, was that they all featured well-known YouTubers – as you might expect at the UK's largest YouTube convention. There was one panel, though, that stood out from the crowd – the smaller YouTubers panel. This featured a group of YouTubers who had fewer subscribers between them than most of the individual 'stars' of SITC – but what they lacked in stats, they made up for in advice and inspiration. Their video audiences may not be huge but the reaction from the crowd at their panel certainly was.

The panel was chaired by Mary Akemon and featured Orla Ainsworth, Aye! Its Aiesha, Ellie Berry, Thogden, Will Carne and SuperSamStuff. The group started off talking about what should truly matter to creators, which then segued into a chat about how important stats are to a YouTuber. Will Carne pointed out that if people take the time to tell you they like something you've made, that means something. Similarly, Sam stated that instead of counting views or likes, he likes to count the number of comments and use that as a measure of how well his videos are doing. The group agreed that analytics can be very useful to a creator, though Ellie noted "you don't have to be this great mathematician" (to make a great video). Thogden summed things up pretty well when he said his favourite thing about YouTube is that you can upload whatever you want. There are no limits. You don't have to follow trends if you don't want to.

The panel ultimately became about community. Mary advised that if you're looking for YouTube pals: 'They're out there, sometimes it just takes a while'. She also warned that it's unrealistic to reach out to people who are "like 50K subs or more" but was confident smaller creators would almost certainly want to help you out. Orla pointed out that everyone started out small, even YouTubers that are huge now. It's the community within the bigger, older YouTubers that has helped them grow.

Sam beautifully summed up the spirit of the day by pointing out that "you're here [at Summer in the City] because you're part of something." He also stated that "there's a misconception that a small YouTuber is a new YouTuber or an unsuccessful YouTuber. Some of us are just happy being smaller. Everyone is working at their own pace", to huge applause from the crowd.

THREE SMALL CREATORS YOU'VE BEEN MISSING OUT ON

LONDON SMALL YOUTUBERS PRESENT SOME OF THEIR HIDDEN GEMS.

If you haven't yet heard of London Small YouTubers, hold onto your socks because we're going to try and knock them off. Affectionately known by many as LSY, they're a local bunch of new media creators, with a hub in London and a passion for YouTube. Call them a community, a fresh-faced start up or a volunteer-squad, to be honest they're all three and more besides. LSY is run by a friendly committee of nine YouTubers who do everything from bringing creator events and opportunities to life to keeping their social media know-how on top form.

In just over a year they went from founder Eleana and a big idea to having an active creator group of almost 600 London-connected members who all love to create, collaborate and connect online and offline.

WHAT EXACTLY DOES LSY DO?

LSY regularly host meet-ups, free training sessions and workshops, socials and sponsored events, and the online Facebook group is always there for members to ask their burning questions. Last year LSY hosted a free workshop evening with certified YouTube marketing experts Derral Eves and David Walsh, moderated panels at Comic Con London, and one of their members won an all-expenses paid trip to VidCon Anaheim through one of LSY's sponsored competitions.

LSY are always eager to shine a light on some much-deserving smaller creators, so take a look below at our current video faves.

AKOS RAJTAMAR

Having moved from Hungary to London, Akos uses his YouTube channel to share travel adventures and updates on how he's getting used to London-living. He always has beautiful footage in his videos, convincing us that you can find beauty everywhere you go. His smart and funny editing style mixed with his catchy and unique music choices always has us clicking play when he uploads.

SHOSH AND MER

Shosh and Mer are a British/American couple living in the UK. This channel is a wonderful haven of chatty vlogs with the main focus on their relationship and LGBTQ+ topics. Their sweet and engaging personalities shine through the screen and make you want to click their next suggested video ASAP.

THE WILKY WAYS

Who doesn't love a family vlogging channel? The Wilky Ways documents the life of the Wilkinson family, originally from England but currently living life in Brussels. Ethan, Joanna and their adorable sons Leo and Noah are delightfully sweet entertainment for when you want to tuck yourself in for some wholesome YouTube viewing.

IS ENOUGH BEING DONE TO KEEP THE YOUTUBE COMMUNITY SAFE?

YouTubers are often expected to be "more accessible" than regular celebrities, but this shouldn't be the case.

In June 2016 the YouTube community was shaken by the senseless killing of musician, inspiration and friend, Christina Grimmie. Making videos on her channel since 2009, Christina had been a valuable member of the community, and had risen to other levels of success such as competing on 'The Voice', touring with Selena Gomez, and landing a promising record deal with Island Records.

Christina's killer was a lone gunman; who had reportedly travelled 100 miles, seemingly with the intent to kill her. She was shot three times, after greeting the shooter at a post-performance signing.

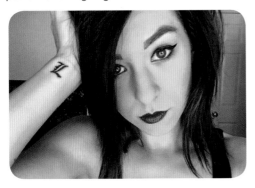

Gun violence is not a new problem for America, and regrettably it isn't even new for the entertainment industry as a whole. But it is a very new potential threat to the YouTube community – and it's still just a worse-case scenario. It is now finally time for YouTube as an industry, the media that surrounds it, and even the fans that support its growth to reconsider just how we view our accessibility to creators.

YouTubers have a relationship with their fans unlike any other form of celebrity. Born on the very social platforms that their audiences use to connect with each other, digital creators thrive on the fact that no matter how big their audiences get, they will always be seen as a part of "Team Internet"; revered as idols, but still just seen as "one of the gang". Sadly, no matter how much we might resist it, the reality is that YouTube is mainstream now – and it's biggest and brightest stars are subject to the same scrutiny, pitfalls and dangers as the celebrities of other media.

Keith
@KeithWOaCrew
Follow

"Gun violence now encroaching on the YouTube community? My community? OUR community?"
@KeithWOaCrew/Twitter

Tremain Hayhoe
@TremainHayhoe
Follow

"Unfortunate truth is higher security, and bodyguards is what YouTubers need. Regular celebs have them. Social media celebs need them."
@TremainHayhoe/Twitter

In recent years, we've seen the necessity for limited, orchestrated and ticketed meet-and-greets for YouTubers increase. And as much as we have all had our reservations about furthering the divide between creators and their audience, it's quickly becoming clear that we need to accept this and evolve much quicker, in order to ensure the safety of influencers everywhere. A lot of this needs to start with the mainstream media, and the way in which they represent YouTubers in their press.

Over the last few years Zoë Sugg and Alfie Deyes have dealt with numerous breaches of privacy as fans and their parents were routinely waiting outside the couples' home in Brighton. We put it to you in an online poll to help us decide who should be blamed the most: the fans; their parents; the media for disclosing the address; or Zoë and Alfie themselves.

The general consensus seemed to be that fans need to be more respectful and understanding of those boundaries – but at this stage, we really need to shine a light on the dangerously flippant way the local and national press have dealt with Zoë and Alfie's pleas for privacy ever since they moved into the house.

Zoë ✔
@Zoella

🔶 Follow   ⌄

"Really starting to lose my patience with people just turning up at our house & peering in or ringing our bell 😩 makes me hate my house!" 😔
@Zoella/Twitter

From the Daily Mail's reveal of their property listing under a headline about Zoella's "£1 million Mansion", to the way that a local paper published their address, it's frightening just what little regard the press seem to have for their privacy. There is also a lot of work to be done internally amidst the YouTube sphere between creators, and how they all present themselves to the wider world to ensure their own safety.

The YouTube community and industry has almost become its own sentient being, growing relentlessly and offering little to no professional training for much of the talent and business that it breeds. And it is quickly becoming apparent that creators – and their respective management – all need to unite on a common idea of just how accessible they wish to continue making themselves, in order to ensure the safety and security of every single creator.

Creators at VidCon who cause stampedes by Tweeting "I'm in the lobby, come find me!" need to be curbed as much as creators attending their own book signing need a security detail that actually understands them and their swarming fans. Some kind of program or class dedicated to security and conduct, instigated by YouTube and the various networks and management centres, could be massively beneficial in ensuring the continued safety of influencers of every platform.

Witnesses say Christina Grimmie prepared to embrace her attacker with open arms. It could have been completely avoided if we offered creators half the respect and security they deserve.

25 INTERNET SLANG WORDS YOU WERE TOO AFRAID TO GOOGLE

WE CAN HELP YOU STAY WOKE, FAM.

Look, we've all been throwing around Internet slang like it's nobody's business, but now it's time to make sure we're all on the same (web)page. We've gathered 25 of the most popular phrases and words that people have stopped using ironically and have been creeping into real life lexicon – so if you've got your reading glasses on, let's open up the library.

AESTHETIC
To have a particular style or vibe that is central to your look, and often works as a form of identification.

BASIC
A way to describe someone who enjoys the most mainstream and predictable things. Lacking originality.

BOOTS
A term added to the end of a sentence to signify some form of emphasis, kind of like a verbal exclamation mark.

DADDY
Two meanings.
1) A partner who takes every good care of you.
2) Someone who has great influence and power over yourself, such as a person you worship or deeply adore.

DEAD/DYING
When something has gone beyond funny that you literally cannot handle it anymore. You've laughed yourself to death.

DONE
To be completely over and finished with something.

EXTRA
To be extremely OTT in every situation even when it's not called for. Often excessive, dramatic or inappropriate.

FAM
An endearing term for your friends, as if you're close family.

FINESSE
To be able to scam, trick and steal under someone's nose in a smooth style.

FR
Acronym for "For Real", used as a full stop to denote that something unbelievable is true.

GOAT
Acronym for "Greatest Of All Time".

GOALS
A phrase used to state that one possesses things (be it fitness, food, relationship, etc.) that they hugely want for themselves. Normally accompanied with a hashtag.

LIT
When something is amazing, popping.

LIVE/LIVING
Experiencing something so incredible that it's making you finally "live". Equally could be said to be giving you "life".

LOW KEY
To keep something a secret or to keep a low profile.

SALT
To state a distinct unhappiness or displeasure at something or someone. Often referred to as "spreading the salt".

SAVAGE
To be the toughest, most lethal person. Can be used in regards to arguments, takedowns and generally having a disregard for the consequences of your words or actions.

SHADE
A way of acting disrespectfully towards a person in a way that notes a level of help. Drag culture sees Queens "throwing shade" at each other for their style, but mostly to help offer edits.

SHIP
To endorse or support a romantic coupling, even if they aren't a reality. Kind of like a fantasy pairing.

SHOOK
To be so completely surprised by something that your body is literally shook. Can also mean you're scared/can't believe your eyes.

SNATCHED
Two meanings.
1) To have incredibly good looks and a body to match, to be so fierce that you look snatched.
2) To burn someone so good that your wig or weave is snatched from your head.

STAN
Often cited as being based on the character from Eminem's music video, this represents a crazy, OTT and often terrifying fan for something (be it a person or a form of media).

THICC
Pronounced either as "tick" or "thicK" (with a heavy K) to refer to a person who is incredibly curvy and attractive. Larger than an hour glass figure.

TRASH
When you exist purely for one thing or person you can be called XXX trash. Also used as a self-deprecating term for being a general mess. This, for example, is one word that because of Internet slang has generated an entirely new meaning.

WOKE
Living in a state of awareness that is above the level of expectation. To be fully aware of current events and the world around them.

THE COMPLETE TIMELINE OF PEWDIEPIE

We're on a trip through time with the most subscribed YouTuber in history.

Whether you subscribe to him or not, it is an undeniable fact that YouTube has been exponentially changed thanks to the presence of PewDiePie. So, with that in mind, here is a breakdown of every single significant moment in his YouTube career. Everyone likes a timeline, right?

2006 DECEMBER 19TH: Felix makes his very first YouTube channel, called "PewDie".

2010 APRIL 29TH: Felix forgets the password to his old YouTube channel, "PewDie", and so starts up a new one called "PewDiePie".

2011 OCTOBER 2ND: The very first video on the PewDiePie channel (that is still live) sees Felix playing Minecraft for two minutes. There is no face cam.

2011 AT SOME POINT IN 2011: Felix drops out of university and works on a hot dog stand whilst focusing on his YouTube career. As soon as he receives his first pay check from Machinima he quits his job. Felix moves to Italy to be with Marzia.

2011 FEBRUARY 17TH: After hitting 100 video uploads and 2,500 subscribers, Felix first shows his face on his YouTube channel in addition to showing off his gaming rig.

2011 SEPTEMBER 2ND: The very first episode of Friday's With PewDiePie is uploaded as Felix decides he wants to be more interactive with his fans. It would go on to separate his channel from other gaming channels, as his personality shines through.

2011 JULY 10TH: The PewDiePie channel reaches its first YouTube milestone of many, with 1 million subscribers.

2012 OCTOBER 25TH: Felix responds to criticism from the media and his fans about his use of 'light-hearted' jokes on serious issues. It's widely considered a good move as Felix shows he's willing to note audience feedback and change his style.

2013 JULY: Felix and Marzia move to Brighton purely for better Internet connection after living in Sweden/Italy and gaining a rapid amount of subscribers.

2013 AUGUST 15TH: PewDiePie becomes the most subscribed to YouTuber in the world, beating Smosh. YouTube Spotlight quickly took the title from Felix, but a day later he took it back and hasn't been rivalled since.

2013 OCTOBER 13TH: He adopts a black pug called Edgar, who has become adored by Felix's audience.

2014 MARCH 3RD: Felix uploads an update vlog where he announces he's scaling back his YouTube output. He feels that uploading every single day is too much for one person and, instead of hiring someone to help, he wants to keep his channel authentic and continue to work solo.

2014 MARCH 29TH: Felix uploads his first 'Goat Simulator Let's Play'. The game becomes a commercial success, thanks to Felix's interest.

2014 AUGUST 29TH: Felix becomes the first (and most popular) YouTuber to switch off comments on his videos for good after making a public statement about how much spam he gets on his channel. The battle between Felix and his comments is still ongoing.

2014 SEPTEMBER 6TH: PewDiePie's YouTube channel became the first to gain over 10 billion video views.

2015 SEPTEMBER 24TH: Felix releases the 'PewDiePie: Legend of the Brofist' app.

2015 OCTOBER 20TH: PewDiePie releases 'This Book Loves You'. It becomes a New York Times Bestseller immediately and remains on the chart for a week.

2015 OCTOBER 21ST: YouTube Red announces Felix's first series, 'Scare PewDiePie', after rumours start surfacing in September that he might be filming a show in LA.

2015 OCTOBER 23RD: On his 26th birthday, Felix hits 40 million subscribers.

2016 JANUARY 13TH: Felix announces his first YouTube network, Revelmode. The network was shutdown early into 2017 after the anti-Semitic controversies.

2016 APRIL 20TH: Time Magazine calls PewDiePie one of the "100 Most Influential People in the World".

2016 JUNE: Felix is evicted from the flat he uses for filming due to being "too loud". He now owns an office space in Brighton where he frequently works with creators such as Emma Pickles and KickThePj.

2016 SEPTEMBER 29TH: Felix releases the successful 'PewDiePie Tuber Simulator' app, where it currently has over 1 million downloads.

2016 OCTOBER 20TH: PewDiePie creates the Jack septiceye2 channel, and it quickly gains over 1.4 million subscribers without any content on it. This channel would prove to be fundamental in one of Felix's later trolls (you know which one I'm on about).

2016 NOVEMBER 15TH: Felix quits his LA vlog series after stress and pressure left him feeling too drained.

2016 DECEMBER 2ND: Felix promises to delete his channel at 50 million subscribers after getting increasingly more annoyed by YouTube not explaining why people were losing subscribers and videos were not being viewed in subscription boxes or recommended bars.

2016 DECEMBER 9TH: Felix doesn't delete his channel (ofc) and trolled us all instead by deleting his Jack septiceye2 "hate" channel.

2016 DECEMBER 12TH: After a weekend of ridiculous live streams and challenges, Revelmode raises $13,000,000 to #EndAIDS with the #Cringemas Xmas event.

2016 DECEMBER 18TH: PewDiePie receives the first Ruby Play Button, which was in the shape of his iconic Brofist logo.

2017 JANUARY 6TH: #PewDiePieIsOverParty trends after Felix edits himself just short of shouting a racial slur in a video. He's accused of not being "allowed" to say that based on his own skin colour.

2017 JANUARY 12TH: In a now privatised video, Felix causes huge controversy by paying two Fiverr users to unscroll an anti-Semitic message. This becomes the catalyst for a later "exposé" by the Wall Street Journal...

2017 FEBRUARY 14TH: ... who publish an article stating that Disney have cut Felix from their network due to anti-Semitic references in his videos. This was the start of a debate between creators and the media after the clips were seemingly "taken out of context" and manipulated to show Felix in a bad light.

2017 FEBRUARY 14TH: On the same day, YouTube announce that they are cancelling season two of 'Scare PewDiePie' due to the ongoing controversy.

2017 MARCH 25TH: Felix uploads an 84-minute long video where he answers questions from a friend. The video is extremely raw and personal and sees Felix discuss topics his fans have never heard him talk about before as well as his thoughts surrounding the Wall Street Journal attacks.

2017 APRIL 10TH: Following YouTube's decision to demonetise channels that aren't "family friendly" (in Felix's words), he announces a new company and Twitch broadcast called "Net Glow".

For a really in-depth look back at PewDiePie's highs and lows, visit **wetheunicorns.com**

QUIZ: MATCH THE YOUTUBER TO THE GOOD DEED

YouTubers are multi-talented beasts; but among their myriad of skills lies the incredible ability to do amazing things for charity. Here are eight instances of YouTubers doing charitable things. But the question is, can you tell which YouTuber did which awesome thing?

Turn to page 93 for the answers!

ZOË & ALFIE

NUMBER: _____

EMMA BLACKERY

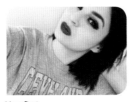

NUMBER: _____

SMOSH

NUMBER: _____

JOHN & HANK GREEN

NUMBER: _____

MARKIPLIER

NUMBER: _____

CONNOR FRANTA

NUMBER: _____

PEWDIEPIE

NUMBER: _____

CARRIE HOPE FLETCHER

NUMBER: _____

1. Which YouTuber raised £1 million for a water charity?

2. Which YouTubers granted wishes for the Rays of Sunshine charity?

3. Which YouTuber donated 12 inches of their hair to charity?

4. Which YouTuber dyed their hair pink for the Depression Bipolar Support Alliance?

5. Which YouTubers created the very successful 'Project For Awesome'?

6. Which YouTuber had their head shaved for charity live on stage at Summer in the City?

7. Which YouTuber raised over $75,000 for The Third Project?

8. Which YouTubers raised $100,000 through their 'Prank It FWD' series?

FIVE TIPS YOU NEED TO KNOW BEFORE GOING TO A YOUTUBE CONVENTION

Here's how to make the most of an amazing – and overwhelming – weekend.

Tons of YouTube conventions happen every year and they can be overwhelming (if you're not appropriately prepared). Luckily for you we've created a simple guide, using our own experience of YouTube events, to make sure you can have the best time possible.

1. PLAN AHEAD

YouTube conventions like Summer in the City and VidCon are huge. You will not be able to do everything you may want to do – at least not all in one day. Events also tend to happen tightly, and can often overlap; so make sure to study the schedule before you go, so that you can make the best use of your time. If you have a good plan you'll be able to have a packed day, without having to rush!

2. HAVE REALISTIC EXPECTATIONS ABOUT MEETING YOUTUBERS

We've heard many a sad tale of a fan or family member of a fan devastated that they haven't been able to meet their favourite YouTuber at an event. Sadly, you're going to have to accept that this is the reality of large-scale meet and greets. YouTubers will try their absolute best to meet everyone they can, but they "art but feeble mortals" and need to sit down eventually just like the rest of us. Keep an open mind about meeting a range of people, instead of just pinning all your hopes on one or two famous ones.

3. REMEMBER TO REST

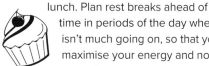

In the rush of the day, you may find that you've been on your feet for hours without realising, or even that you've forgotten to have lunch. Plan rest breaks ahead of time in periods of the day when there isn't much going on, so that you can maximise your energy and not burn out too early.

4. GET THAT GUARDIAN A COFFEE AND A CHAIR

Parents and guardians can have a rough time at these conventions. There's a good chance that they will be confused by the whole thing so make sure to find them a good chair and a steady source of coffee and snacks.

5. REMEMBER TO HAVE FUN!

Big events can be overwhelming, especially with the amount of people attending, the number of things to do and the possibility of meeting your favourite YouTubers. We're not being cheesy when we say – don't forget to take a minute to soak it all up! These events are pretty infrequent, so while you're in the eye of the storm, you might as well make the most of it. Good luck – and have fun!

GROWING UP AND GROWING OUT OF YOUR FAVOURITE YOUTUBERS

YOUTUBE HAS BEEN AROUND FOR A LONG TIME, AND IT'S ONLY NATURAL WE DON'T LOVE THE SAME PEOPLE WE USED TO.

YouTube has been around for over 11 years now. And that means we've seen literally countless hours of content uploaded, hundreds of thousands of creators upload their videos, and hundreds of YouTubers become household names across the world; building on their viral success and becoming global business men and women. For many of us, we've been watching YouTube for somewhere between 5-10 years, and we've seen the platform change and grow. From the very first video we watched to cheering on their milestones, we all remember just which creators got us hooked on the platform. But are they still the same ones you love today? And how does it feel when you've genuinely moved on?

Whilst most mainstream YouTubers will talk about how their audiences are aged 18-24, you only have to take to social media to see the masses of very young children enjoying their content; and attending things like meet-ups and book signings. It can often appear that some YouTubers create content for a younger audience – one which will buy their merchandise in droves, and be loyal fans on social media.

As a result, fans in their mid-twenties and onwards can often feel like the creators we started watching and loved "back in the day" are no longer creating content for us.

SO WE FIND NEW CREATORS

It sounds so simple, but you can get into a slump, watching the same people you've watched for years, sometimes not even enjoying or engaging with their content. And finding new creators can seem so difficult. Luckily for you, we've created a ton of content to help you. Go to page 59 for some brilliant smaller creators, or check out wetheunicorns.com – we're always sharing our favourite, new creators.

YOU CAN STILL SUPPORT YOUR OLD FAVES AND NOT ENJOY THEIR CONTENT

We all have creators we once enjoyed, but no longer rush to the platform to watch their latest videos. But not wanting to press the unsub button, they sit in our subscription boxes feeling like a sad old teddy bear we no longer play with. But you can absolutely unsub to them without feeling bad and support their growing empire in other ways.

When Louise Pentland spoke out about wanting to make her channel more grown up, she faced criticism for creating content of a more adult nature. If you're a die-hard fan of

Louise's old content – lighter and less adult – and you're not so keen on the new stuff, there's no reason to ridicule and shout down the creator for their new direction. Instead, if you still want to be supportive but aren't interested in what they have to say then why not follow them on social media or check out what else they're doing? Maybe, like Louise, they're releasing a book that might be more your style or perhaps their Pinterest account or Insta is where you can get your fix.

TELL YOUR FAVOURITE YOUTUBER WHAT YOU WANT TO SEE

Unlike most jobs, YouTubers don't have weekly meetings with their boss or a yearly review. For creators, their work is based on feedback from their audience, their strategy and plan for their channel – and of course, what is getting the most views. But if you don't speak up then how are they supposed to know that they're missing out on potentially millions of views?

Loved that minimal makeup look they did? Let them know. A fan of their lookbook? Holla. Positive feedback and constructive criticism is incredibly helpful to creators and the majority are more than open to listening to you and working on their output.

FINALLY, ACCEPT IT AND MOVE ON

Trust us, we've all had to unsub from a creator we once loved, and it absolutely sucks. Whether they've turned "problematic" or you've outgrown them, it's not the best feeling to say goodbye to someone you've watched for years, and who essentially feels like a friend. But as with a lot of friendships, there are times when you just need to switch off and say goodbye – and that absolutely goes for creators, too.

Sad times.

WHAT IT REALLY MEANS TO BE A YOUTUBE TROLL

They love it when we hate them – but why?

Another week, another troll; it's a tale as old as time: a person comes along and generates huge amounts of publicity by being Hashtag Controversial; whipping everyone up into a small frenzy. The matter of whether or not the person in question genuinely believes the things they say becomes irrelevant because they're playing on reaction rather than actually pushing a message. These figures have long existed in politics and on TV, but until recently they have not found significant status on YouTube. Now a new breed of uber-troll is rising, much to the general annoyance and boredom of people everywhere.

Figures like Nicole Arbour, the newly-arrived Hunter Avallone and others thrive on being as controversial and 'straight-talking' as possible. They position themselves as the voice of the 'hard truths' of the world and seem to drink-in backlash as if it fuels them, or somehow proves them right.

THE VETERAN

You're probably sick to death of hearing about Nicole Arbour of 'Dear Fat People' fame but it's worth mentioning her for a second as she is arguably the poster child for a YouTube troll. She posts rants that she has scientifically-engineered to be as controversial as possible, in order to generate hype (albeit negative about herself) and in turn increase her status

and, presumably, YouTube income.

It's an interesting development on a platform that is traditionally so focused on personality and personal branding. Whereas vloggers have built empires upon being relatable and likeable, figures like Nicole build channels (ultimately) around being unlikeable. It's a strategy that can be lucrative in the short term but lacks long-term potential. Fans will follow a YouTuber they love for years – but how long will people follow a YouTuber they hate? It's not a viable long game.

MISSPENT YOUTH

You may not have heard of Hunter Avallone. He's an American teen who recently caused a stir with a video that roundly denounced transsexuals (you honestly don't need to watch it, it's exactly what you'd expect). It's not clear what Hunter is really trying to achieve with this video. It sparked the age-old question of 'yes you can do this, but should you?'

Trans people are hardly a group that are broadly accepted (yet) by society or who enjoy any advantages over other groups of people. Instead they face widespread bullying, derision and have a very high risk of suicide, especially among young people. Why he decided that this was the group that needed to be brought down a peg or two just doesn't seem very clear. What is clear is that he did not get a universally warm response to his video.

If you visit his Twitter, you see that Avallone routinely retweets people who support him. This does not give the impression of someone who doesn't care about people's opinions of him. It appears to present someone who does care and who is finding solace in people's support in the face of a backlash that might be unsettling for him. No matter how hard-hearted Hunter may claim to be, can a 19 year-old stare into the void of hundreds of strangers calling him a bigot and not feel anything at all? It may not be regret he feels, but it will be something. He's only human after all.

Ultimately Avallone is young and may not fully understand the consequences of what he is doing. For example: in an age where nothing can ever be truly deleted from the Internet, it may hurt his future employment prospects if there is a video of him online

where he expresses bigoted views against a vulnerable group. I honestly wonder how much he has thought about this – after all, it is common for people to make short-sighted decisions when they're young and foolish. If he were reading this, though, I would ask him: as a young person, do you really want the world to define you as a figure of hatred? It doesn't seem like a happy existence.

Nicole gets no sympathy, though. She is a grown woman making deliberately inflammatory (and short-sighted) decisions and she is now, rightfully, paying the price. Her shock value has dwindled and her appeal as a troll has grown tired. Basically: no one cares any more.

In the age of the Internet, the question always seems to be whether someone can and should do something. Whenever anyone's statements are questioned they always spring to the argument that they have freedom of speech and can say what they want. This lacks the nuance of the real world, though. Don't ask can I say this – ask yourself should I say this? Will me saying this achieve anything productive? Will me saying this stuff just bring more sadness and misery into the world? You have to stop and ask whether being a hub for hatred and unhappiness is really the persona you want for yourself, because at the very least, it can't be a state of being that leaves you very happy. Does Nicole Arbour ever look truly happy in her videos? She looks defiant, she looks defensive – but there's no happiness there. How can there be when your name is synonymous with anger and bullying?

QUIZ: CAN YOU GUESS THE LILLY SINGH VIDEO FROM THE OBSCURE QUOTE?

"MY HOURS ARE VERY CLEAR OKAY? 12PM UNTIL I GET TIRED."

We already know just how quotable many YouTubers are. Some are motivational, while some are inexplicably worth reviewing candles with. But nearly all of our favourite YouTubers' best quotes come from their videos, with no context; and Lilly Singh is no exception. Lilly is full of brilliant quotes that are inspirational, relatable, and just weird out of context. We've yanked some Lilly quotes out of their original context – but can you figure out which video they belong to?

1 "When you don't put the seat down, it's like... no-scope rekt pwn'd exsanguinated me brah?"

Types Of Kids At School

How To Date a Gamer

2 "Their booty looking so right, they could never make a left turn without hitting a pedestrian."

The 6 Stages of Having a Crush

Types Of Flirting

3 "What is this? A flotation device?!"

#LEH

Types of Commercials

4 "There was so much traffic on the highway."

What I Do On Airplanes

How Girls Get Ready...

90

Turn to page 93 for the answers!

5 "You don't deserve the flask!"

[ ] The Difference Between Brown and White Girls

[ ] Types of Parents

6 "My hours are very clear, okay? 12pm until I get tired."

[ ] How I Get Work Done

[ ] How To Be a YouTube Star

7 "I'm not really sure y'all wanted this collab to happen."

[ ] What Clubbing Is Actually Like

[ ] The Rule of Racism

8 "You asking why I need my own slipper? To beat your head!"

[ ] How I Clean My Room

[ ] How My Parents See Things...

THE FUTURE OF YOUTUBE

WHAT'S ON THE CARDS FOR YOUTUBE IN THE COMING YEARS? IT'S IN YOUR HANDS!

Over the course of this book we have explored many corners of the world of YouTube — and the best part is, we've barely scratched the surface. As the online community continues to grow, there will be boundless creativity; more chances for new ideas and new friendships. Perhaps we will see a new feat of skill that will make the Bottle Flip look like child's play; perhaps we'll meet a new unlikely hero who will put Damn Daniel to shame. Perhaps Dan Howell will do something hilariously awkward (actually, that's definitely going to happen). The steps forward for the world of YouTube will be taken by the people who have always made YouTube as magical as it is: the creators and the fans. The people who make, and the people who support. There has never been a form of media more inclusive and more collaborative. It is people like you — people who live and breathe YouTube, people who want to make cool stuff and to see cool stuff, you are the people that will carry this community into the next century and beyond. What is the future of YouTube? The future is you. So, get out there and do something awesome.

PAGE 12-13
QUIZ: How Well Do You Remember YouTube In 2008?
1. **b. lonelygirl15** Revealed to be a hoax in 2006, LG15 finally ended its story in 2008!
2. **a. Gangs** FiveAwesomeGoats was VERY real.
3. **c. 888** It was hosted on August 8th in Toronto by Corey Vidal.
4. **b. Phil** Dan's channel didn't exist. He is a YOUTUBE BABY.
5. **b. Evolution of Dance** It was one of the original viral videos!
6. **a. The Partner Program** YouTubers started making that sweet advertising money this year.
7. **a. thelonelyisland** They were INESCAPABLE.
8. **c. 100,000** Charlie was the first UK YouTuber to reach this milestone!

PAGE 29
QUIZ: Do You Know The YouTubers' Real Names?
jacksepticeye: Seán William McLoughlin
grav3yardgirl: Bunny Meyer
PointlessBlog: Alfie Deyes
danisnotonfire: Daniel Howell
Lohanthony: Anthony Quintal
Wheezywaiter: Craig Benzine
SeaNanners: Adam Montoya
Jenna Marbles: Jenna Mourey
PsychoSoprano: Colleen Ballinger

PAGE 42-43
QUIZ: Which Of These YouTubers Have NOT Collabed?
1. **a.** Jon Cozart
2. **a.** KSI
3. **a.** Scola Dondo
4. **a.** Brizzy Voices
5. **b.** Laci Green
6. **c.** Zoella
7. **b.** Meghan Tonjes
8. **c.** BananaJamana
9. **b.** TomSka
10. **a.** Savannah Brown

PAGE 52-53
QUIZ: Can You Guess These YouTubers From Our Terrible Drawings?
1. **c.** Zoë Sugg
2. **a.** Dan Howell
3. **c.** Tyler Oakley
4. **a.** Nathan Zed
5. **b.** Dodie Clark
6. **b.** Miranda Sings
7. **c.** Phil Lester

PAGE 56-57
QUIZ: Can You Spot Which YouTuber Is The Odd One Out?
1. **c. Anna Saccone** – the other two have Netflix Originals
2. **b. Sophie Foster** is the only one who's English
3. **b. David Dobrik** – the other two are lifestyle vloggers
4. **a. Mark Ferris** – the other two haven't appeared in music videos
5. **a. Joey Graceffa** – the other two are pranksters
6. **c. Emma Blackery** – she has never starred in a film
7. **a.** That one was easy! **Markiplier** isn't a beauty YouTuber
8. **a. Sean Elliott OC** doesn't have a pet (yet!)

PAGE 60-61
QUIZ: Is This A Screenshot From A Dan Video, Or A Phil Video?
1. **This is a Phil video:** 'WILL DAN AND PHIL SURVIVE AUSTRALIA?'
2. **This is a Dan video:** 'Audience Participation Fear'
3. **This is a Dan video:** 'DAN IS ON FIRE'
4. **This is a Phil video:** 'THE FUTURE QUIZ! (with KickThePj)'
5. **This is a Phil video:** 'Phil learns to sing!'
6. **This is a Dan video:** 'That Charity Advert'
7. **This is a Dan video:** 'The Dan and Phil 3D AUDIO EXPERIENCE (Audiobook Trailer!) '

PAGE 69
QUIZ: Can You Match The YouTuber To The Country They Were Born In?
1. Flula Borg was born in Germany
2. Lilly Singh was born in Canada
3. Marzia Bisognin was born in in Italy
4. PewDiePie was born in Sweden
5. Anna Saccone was born in the USA
6. Caspar Lee was born in England
7. Troye Sivan was born in South Africa
8. Liam Dryden was born in Scotland
9. Darude was born in Finland

PAGE 84
QUIZ: Match The YouTuber To The Good Deed
1. PewDiePie raised £1 million for a water charity
2. Zoë and Alfie granted wishes for the Rays of Sunshine charity
3. Carrie Hope Fletcher donated 12 inches of her hair to charity
4. Markiplier dyed his hair pink for the Depression Bipolar Support Alliance
5. John and Hank Green created the very successful 'Project For Awesome'
6. Emma Blackery had her head shaved for charity live on stage at Summer in the City
7. Connor Franta raised over $75,000 for The Third Project
8. Smosh raised $100,000 through their 'Prank It FWD' series

PAGE 90-91
QUIZ: Can You Guess The Lilly Singh Video From The Obscure Quote?
1. Types Of Kids At School
2. The 6 Stages of Having a Crush
3. #LEH
4. How Girls Get Ready...
5. Types of Parents
6. How To Be a YouTube Star
7. What Clubbing Is Actually Like
8. How I Clean My Room

CREDITS AND ACKNOWLEDGEMENTS

Picture Credits

Copyright of the images remains with the individuals and organisations credited below. Every effort has been made to trace the copyright holders and to obtain their permission for use of copyrighted material. If any accidental omission or error has been made, the publishers will be pleased to rectify this in future editions of this book.

(T = top, B = bottom, L = left, R = right, C= centre)

Cover

TC © DFree/Shutterstock; BC © Featureflash Photo Agency/Shutterstock; TL, TR, CL © Kathy Hutchins/Shutterstock; BL © Lauren Elisabeth/Shutterstock; BR © Tinseltown/Shutterstock.

Interiors

YouTube:

59TL © Abi Spear Soprano/YouTube; 76BL © Akos Rajtmar/YouTube; 8TL, 8TC, 8BL, 9CR, 9BR, 12BR, 36#1, 48BL, 60#1, 60#4, 61#5, 92BL © AmazingPhil/YouTube; 41CL © Anna Akana/YouTube; 17BC © BBC News/YouTube; 9TL © BBC Radio 1/YouTube; 66BR © Benjaminoftomes/YouTube; 67TL © Books Beauty Ameriie/YouTube; 67CR © booksandquills/YouTube; 50BR © CaseyNeistat/YouTube; 1CR, 4TR, 39BL, 70CL, 70CR © Caspar/YouTube; 59TC © catiewahwah/YouTube; 13BR © charlieissocoollike/YouTube; 73TL © charlieissocoollike/YouTube; 67CL © Charr Frears/YouTube; 32#32 © ConnorFranta/YouTube; 12BL © Corey Vidal/YouTube; 35#8 © Corridor/YouTube; 59TR © Creative Reindeer/YouTube; 42#2b © Cryaotic/YouTube; 9TC, 16CR, 74TR, 74CR, 74BR © DanAndPhilGAMES/YouTube; 8BL, 8BC, 9TR, 60#2, 60#3, 61#6, 61#7 © Daniel Howell/YouTube; 59CL © dizzybrunette3/YouTube; 80TL © doddleoddle/YouTube; 39TR © doddlevloggle/YouTube; 39CR © Elijah & Christine/YouTube; 8TR © Emily Claire/YouTube; 59BC © Emma Inks/YouTube; 36#3 © FilmCow/YouTube; 59BC © Full Flourish/YouTube; 32#35, 59BL © GoldVision/YouTube; 66BL © GoWithFlick/YouTube; 46TC, 65BC, 87TR © Grace F Victory/YouTube; 44TR © Hey Its Emily/YouTube; 89TL © Hunter Avallone/YouTube; 16CR © IHasCupQuake/Instagram; 1BR, 40TR, 80TR, 90#1L, 90#1R, 90#2L, 90#2R, 90#3L, 90#3R, 90#4L, 90#4R, 91T, 91#5L, 91#5R, 91#6L, 91#6R, 91#7L, 91#7R, 91#8L, 91#8R © IISupermanII/YouTube; 33#27 © Ingrid Nilsen/YouTube; 46BC © It's Em/YouTube; 32#33 © ItsWayPastMyBedTime/YouTube; 75TL © itswillcarne/YouTube; 39CL © Jack & Dean/YouTube; 22TR © Jack Howard/YouTube; 40BR © JackConteExtras/YouTube; 34#16, 38TL © jacksepticeye/YouTube; 31#44 © JAGGL113/YouTube; 59TR © jameboyy/YouTube; 36#4 © jawed/YouTube; 67BR © Jean Bookishthoughts/YouTube; 66TR © Jen Campbell/YouTube; 59BR © JK FLASH/YouTube; 35#6 © Joe/YouTube; 34#20 © JusReign/YouTube; 67BL © Katie Ruby/YouTube; 33#24 © KickThePj/YouTube; 59TC © Kite Visionary/YouTube; 42#2a © KSI/YouTube; 65BL © lacigreen/YouTube; 12TR © Lauren Fairweather/YouTube; 38BR, 44TL, 92CR © Liza Koshy/YouTube; 39TL © Logo_TodrickHall/YouTube; 44BL © Lucy Wood/YouTube; 87BR © Marcus Butler/YouTube; 80BL © Mark Ferris/YouTube; 26CL, 35#13 © markiplier/YouTube; 75TR © maryakemon/YouTube; 59BR © Match Not Found/YouTube; 17TL © Matt Little/YouTube; 44BR © Mikhila McDaid/YouTube; 59C © millymollymandy16/YouTube; 34#18, 37TR, 37CL, 37CR, 37BR, 37BR © Miranda Sings/YouTube; 44TC © MsRosieBea/YouTube; 17TR, 33#25 © MyHarto/YouTube; 31#40 © Neil Cicierega/YouTube; 88BL © Nicole Arbour/YouTube; 35#11 © nigahiga/YouTube; 36#5 © OkGoVEVO/YouTube; 71CL, 71CR © Oli White/YouTube; 75CR © orlaainsworth/YouTube; 34#15 © Paint/YouTube; 18CR, 24TL, 38TR © Patricia Bright/YouTube; 17BL, 24BR, 50TL, 58TR, 62T, 62BR, 83C, 92TR © PewDiePie/YouTube; 18BR, 80CR © PointlessBlogVlogs/YouTube; 12TL © Red Vs Blue/YouTube; 30#50 © RickAstleyVEVO/YouTube; 13TR © RiyadhK/YouTube; 44BC © Robyn Eede/YouTube; 67TR © Rose Reads/YouTube; 32#30 © SACCONEJOLYs/YouTube; 51BR © Scola Dondo/YouTube; 59TC © SeekND FPV/YouTube; 51TL © shane/YouTube; 77TR © Shosh and Mer/YouTube; 86BR © Smosh/YouTube; 33#22, 38BL, 46CR, 64TL, 71TL, 71TR, 87CL © Sprinkleofglitter/YouTube; 66TL © sunbeamsjess/YouTube; 4CR. 31#41 © Tanya Burr/YouTube; 13TL, 30#47 © TayZonday/YouTube; 70BL, 70BR © ThatcherJoe/YouTube; 38CR © The Gabbie Show/YouTube; 59TL © The Unifiers/YouTube; 77BL © The Wilky Ways/YouTube; 13BL © thelonelyisland/YouTube; 39BR © Thomas Sanders/YouTube; 31#37 © TomSka/YouTube; 38CL, 63TL, 65BR, 81BL © Tyler Oakley/YouTube; 20BL, 21CL © VidCon/YouTube; 14CL, 14TC © YouTube Spotlight/YouTube; 59CL © zarastuart89/YouTube; 36#2, 70TL, 70TR © Zoella/YouTube.

Instagram:

16CR © amberjames862657/Instagram; 57#6a © annaakana/Instagram; 56#1c © annasaccone/Instagram; 84TCR © anthonypadilla/Instagram; 17TC © ashleeebs/Instagram; 43#8c © bananajamana/Instagram; 42#4a © brizzyvoices/Instagram; 56#1b © camerondallas/Instagram; 17BL © canon.aph.poland/Instagram; 43#7a, 84BR © carriehopefletcher/Instagram; 11BC, 69TC © caspar_lee/Instagram; 17TC © cheechunnnnn/Instagram; 29BR, 43#5a © colleen/Instagram; 84BCL © connorfranta/Instagram; 1BL, 23TR, 29CL © danisnotonfire/Instagram; 43#9b, 71BR © darksquidge/Instagram; 56#3b © daviddobrik/Instagram; 57#6c, 84TCL © emmablackery/Instagram; 43#6b © fleurdeforce/Instagram; 43#6a © gracefvictory/Instagram; 43#8a © gracehelbig/Instagram; 1C, 29TC © grav3yardgirl/Instagram; 5CR, 19TR © iisupermanii/Instagram; 56#3a © inthefrow/Instagram; 5BR, 42#2c, 69TL, 82C © itsmarziapie/Instagram; 42#4c © itsmikeymurphy/Instagram; 43#7c © jackhoward/Instagram; 29TL © jacksepticeye/Instagram; 29BC © jennamarbles/Instagram; 57#5c

94

© jessewelle/Instagram; 47BR © joe_sugg/Instagram; 57#5a © joeygraceffa/Instagram; 84TR © johngreenwritesbooks/Instagram; 42#1a, 43#8b © joncozart/Instagram; 43#10c © jusreign/Instagram; 42#1c © kingsleyyy/Instagram; 43#5b © lacigreen/Instagram; 69TR © liamdryden/Instagram; 56#2c © lizakoshy/Instagram; 29C © lohanthony/Instagram; 57#7b © mannymua733/Instagram; 57#7a, 84BL © markipliergram/Instagram; 56#4a © markyferris/Instagram; 43#7b © meghantonjes/Instagram; 42#3b © meowitslucy/Instagram; 57#7c © michellephan/Instagram; 16TL, 16BL, 47TL, 56#1a © mirandasingsofficial/Instagram; 42#3c © mrtimh/Instagram; 43#9a © nathanzed/Instagram; 68TR, 82TR, 84BCR © pewdiepie/Instagram; 54BR, 55CL, 92C, 92BR © playlistlive/Instagram; 25TR, 29TR, 84TL © pointlessblog/Instagram; 43#10b © realjacksfilms/Instagram; 57#5b © romanatwood/Instagram; 56#2a © safiyany/Instagram; 56#3c © samanthamariaofficial/Instagram; 43#10a © savannahb/Instagram; 42#3a © scoladondo/Instagram; 29BL © seananners/Instagram; 57#8a © seanelliotoc/Instagram; 43#5c © selenagomez/Instagram; 56#4c © shirleybeniang/Instagram; 54TL, 54BL © sitc_event/ Instagram; 56#2b © sophie_fosterxx/Instagram; 42#4b © strawburry17/Instagram; 42#1b, 57#8c © tanyaburr/Instagram; 56#4b © thepatriciabright/Instagram; 78CL © therealgrimmie/Instagram; 21CR © thomassanders/Instagram; 57#6b © troyesivan/Instagram; 47BL © tyleroakley/Instagram; 43#9c © unge/Instagram; 57#8b © velvetgh0st/Instagram; 85TL © vidcon/Instagram; 29CR © wheezywaiter/ Instagram; 1CL, 11BL, 43#6c, 47TR, 72BR, 78CL, 92TL © zoella/Instagram; 48BC © zoellalifestyle/Instagram.

Twitter:

9BL, 9BC, 9CL © AmazingPhil/Twitter; 45TR © atwooddawson/Twitter; 65CR © BeckieJBrown/Twitter; 45BL © brokeangel/Twitter; 64BR © CallieThorpe/Twitter; 45BR © ChaseButlerTV/Twitter; 65TL © GraceFVictory/Twitter; 65CR © HeyRowanEllis/Twitter; 45TL © httpzouwee/Twitter; 64BL © jakeftmagic/Twitter; 78CR © KeithWOaCrew/Twitter; 65TR © lexcanroar/Twitter; 63CR © MadeULookbyLex/ Twitter; 15TR © OhLookItsAKyle/Twitter; 15CL © Oona_King/Twitter; 64CL, 65CL © papertimelady/Twitter; 14TR © sulibreaks/ Twitter; 71BL, 73TR © thetomska/Twitter; 78BR © TremainHayhoe/Twitter; 64TL © tyleroakley/Twitter; 72TL, 78BL © Zoella/Twitter.

Shutterstock:

17BR © aimy27feb/Shutterstock; 17BC © AlexKZ/Shutterstock; 17BC © Anan Kaewkhammul/Shutterstock; 28BR © Aratehortua/ Shutterstock; 17TL © bestv/Shutterstock; 16BR © Christina Henningstad/Shutterstock; 17CL © elbud/Shutterstock; 69BC © EPS10J/ Shutterstock; 17CL © grafvision/Shutterstock; 16CL © gresi/Shutterstock; 16CL © HarisEna/Shutterstock; 17BC © Ilya Chalyuk/ Shutterstock; 69CL © Jeerasak banditram/Shutterstock; 81CR © Jstone/Shutterstock; 69BL © Julia Sanders/Shutterstock; 69CR © Loveshop/Shutterstock; 17BR © Lucy Liu/Shutterstock; 69C, 69C, 69BR © Maximumvector/Shutterstock; 69CL, 69CR © petch one/ Shutterstock; 16TR © Runrun2/Shutterstock; 16CL © SimpleEPS/Shutterstock; 88TR © Stockforliving/Shutterstock; 17BR © Yuliya Evstratenko/Shutterstock.

Map illustrations by Julia Scheele
Emoji illustrations by Bernard Chau
Doodle illustrations by Crazy Monkey Creative
All other images, including YouTube logo courtesy of Shutterstock.com.

Studio Press and **wetheunicorns.com** would like to thank the following people:

Michaela Walters, Megan Wastell, Steve Wilson-Beales, Hollie Brooks, Liam Dryden, Benedict Townsend and Charleyy Hodson.